AMERICAN LITERATURE LIFEPAC 4
THE MODERN AGE 1915–1946

CONTENTS

I. **THE MODERN AGE** 1

    MODERN PROSE 7

    Ernest Hemingway 7

    F. Scott Fitzgerald 12

II. **MODERN POETRY** 32

    Ezra Pound 32

    Carl Sandburg 33

    E. E. Cummings 35

    Wallace Stevens 38

    Robert Frost 40

    W. H. Auden 42

III. **OTHER MODERN AGE LITERATURE** 47

    HARLEM RENAISSANCE — Langston Hughes 47

    DRAMA — Thornton Wilder 49

    RELIGIOUS WORKS — J. Gresham Machen 51

Author: **Krista L. White, B.S.**

Editor: Alan Christopherson, M.S.

Graphic Design: Lauren Durain, A.S.T.

Alpha Omega Publications®

804 N. 2nd Ave. E., Rock Rapids, IA 51246-1759

Alpha Omega Publications, Inc.

804 N. 2nd Ave. E., Rock Rapids, IA 51246-1759
© MM, All rights reserved.

AMERICAN LITERATURE LIFEPAC 4
1914–1946

OBJECTIVES:

1. Gain an overview of the history and dominant ideas of the modern era.
2. Discern the influence of modernism upon religion and the arts.
3. Identify the elements of modernism in American literature.
4. Recognize Christianity's answers to modern problems.

VOCABULARY:

apparition - a starting appearance
chaos - confusion and disorder
culminate - to end or stop at highest point
discontinuity - a break or lack of connection
grave - serious; important
inerrant - without error
mundane - ordinary
obstinate - stubborn; unable to turn
preposterous - absurd or ridiculous
replete - filled abundantly
theology - the study of God
unconventional - not the norm; unusual
wanton - without regard for what is right; senseless

I. THE MODERN AGE

The Modern Era. Gertrude Stein, one of the most influential writers and thinkers of the modern era, said of her purpose and place in history, "I was there to kill what was not dead, the nineteenth century, which was so sure of evolution and prayers." The "modern temper" was uncertain and distrustful of science and religion. World War I proved that society had failed. Civilization, aided by its technological advances, seemed to destroy itself. For the first time, one man equipped with a machine gun could instantly send a dozen men to their eternal domain. War was no longer an exercise in honor and courage but a swirl of mass destruction where only the "lucky" survived. Life seemed meaningless and chaotic. In the face of such bloodshed and torment, people forgot, dismissed, and scorned God and His sovereign rule. In the period between World War I and World War II, writers like Stein searched for meaning in art. Their culminating rejection of biblical Christianity left society disoriented and fearful.

"The War to End All Wars." On July 28, 1914, the heir-apparent of Austria and Hungry, Archduke Francis Ferdinand, was assassinated by a Serb nationalist. The killing was the result of the growing nationalism within Europe. Nationalism was the intense desire to establish independent states within Europe based on ethnic origins. This movement favored democracy. The American and French revolutions were strong incentives to overthrow or put down the existing political and economic structures, which were based on imperial rule. The whole world was pushing toward change.

The war between Austria and Serbia soon became a worldwide struggle for political, economic, and military supremacy. The thirty-two nations involved were divided into two coalitions. The Central Powers consisted of Germany, Austria, Turkey, and Bulgaria. Initially, the Allies consisted of Great Britain, France, Russia, and Italy.

Both before and after the war, America was reluctant to involve itself in the affairs of the Old World. For most of the war, the United States acted as an arbitrator between the two powers. President Woodrow Wilson labored for peace, but when Germany threatened to destroy Great Britain's shipping industry, the United States could no longer remain neutral. On April 6, 1917, Congress declared war on Germany and joined the Allied cause.

The United States' involvement in World War I elevated the nation to a position of world power. The large-scale loss of life witnessed by many writers caused a pessimism that would cloud the nation's conscience for years to follow. As William Dean Howells had prefigured in his short story "Editha," modern war was not glorious. Conflict resulted in death and pain, not honor.

Feelings of discontentment with traditional manners and beliefs followed the war. America felt betrayed. The old had failed. Broken and wounded, the nation turned to a new order. Rising affluence, the pursuit of pleasure, and the deterioration of morality characterized the decade that followed World War I.

The Jazz Age. The 1920s were known as the Jazz Age, or the Roaring Twenties. Many forces contributed to the social upheaval experienced by the United States after World War I. Industrialization had moved people out of small rural communities and into the big cities of the East and Midwest. Within a short period of time, America became an urban nation colored with the cultures and lifestyles of immigrants from Eastern European nations. In addition to the changes in social structure were advances in communication and transportation.

The inventions of the nineteenth century—such as the record player, radio, and the motion picture—made their way into the lives of the average American. The advent of mass communication created a new culture called popular (or "pop") culture. Radio and film connected the centers of sophistication and wealth with the poorer, less advantaged parts of the nation. A farm girl in rural Kentucky could easily know the latest fashions in Hollywood or New York City by watching a motion picture at her local theatre. These new connections helped to spread the desire for social permissiveness and the pursuit of pleasure. During this time, fads in dress and behavior leaped into existence.

The automobile also had a profound effect on American society and culture. With its ability to move people far away from their roots, the automobile only added to the turbulence in society. By 1920, the automobile was affordable to most Americans, causing changes to both the workforce and urban development. Suburbs sprung up around the major cities. People preferring to live outside the city commuted into the cities for work each day. The demand for a more mobile lifestyle also created more jobs. Automobile plants, steel mills, highway construction crews, and gas stations provided the nation with new occupations.

The Eighteenth Amendment to the U.S. Constitution—the prohibition of the manufacture and sale of alcohol—had the effect of pushing America further toward the edge of decadence and disintegration. This well-meant attempt by social reformers and religious groups to control the unraveling of the nation's moral fabric only backfired. With the imposed restrictions, society seemed to enjoy the taste of intoxicating liquors even more and Victorian standards of behavior even less. Organized crime offered normally law-abiding citizens places to drink called "speakeasies." These illegal bars and taverns also exposed many people to the darker pleasures of the streets, namely, prostitution.

Some people sometimes viewed the gangster as a hero; other people viewed him as a villain. He provided the people with what they wanted, but his services also required acts of extortion and bloodshed. Warfare between gangs occupied the headlines of most major city newspapers. Police officers and other law enforcement officials who were unwilling to uphold the Eighteenth Amendment often turned a blind eye to gang activities. Prohibition was largely ignored. In 1933, it was repealed.

"The New Woman." The pursuit of pleasure was not limited to a swig of whiskey or a bottle of beer. During the 1920s, American society opened its arms to the "flapper," a woman

2

who behaved in a morally unrestrained manner. Her behavior was popularized by a dance called the Charleston. People across the nation watched as beautiful, scantily dressed women danced wildly across the movie screen. The movements of the Charleston were provocative and strikingly different from the ballroom dances of the past.

These changes in sexual behavior followed closely on the heels of the Nineteenth Amendment to the U.S. Constitution. In August 1920, the Nineteenth Amendment to the Constitution was ratified giving women the right to vote. The women's suffrage movement, which found its roots in the revivals of the Second Great Awakening, had finally borne fruit. Political freedom opened the doors to occupational and educational independence. Women entered the workforce in places that were once reserved only for men. Seeking greater independence, they left the limits of home to become business executives, lawyers, doctors, and college professors.

Science and Culture. The impact of Darwinism and its reduction of man to a mere animal driven and controlled by desires continued to have an effect on society. Sigmund Freud (1856–1939), considered the father of psychology, introduced a view of man that reduced him to little more than the outworking of suppressed sexual desires. Freud theorized that all of man's problems stem from unsatisfied desires. He distinguished the conscious from the subconscious, the conscious being the thinking part of the human mind, while the subconscious being the desire-driven part of the mind. He taught that to be psychologically healthy, one should allow the subconscious to control their behavior. The satisfaction of lustful desires was justified as "needful" to one's sanity. Freud's antibiblical theories encouraged the decline of social and personal morality. One writer noted that people now had a "scientific" excuse for their sexual immorality.

Bread line–Great Depression

The Great Depression. In October 1929, the Roaring Twenties came to a sudden end. The jazz players exchanged their lively tunes for a solitary cry: "Brother, Can You Spare a Dime?" The stock market crash left millions of people jobless and hungry. As banks closed, thousands of people lost their farms, their homes, and their life's savings. By 1932, more than 25 percent of the nation's workers were unemployed.

The increasing number of bread lines trailing out of soup kitchens led many people to doubt the wisdom of capitalism. Some people, desperate for answers, turned to the economic theories of Karl Marx, the father of communism. During the 1930s, communism enjoyed popularity among union workers and the intellectual elite. Members of the American Communist Party believed that industrial production in the hands of the worker would yield a more stable economic system. They blamed free enterprise for the turmoil of the 1930s and promised prosperity for all.

In 1932 Franklin Delano Roosevelt was elected president. To avoid possible revolution that would bring America to its knees, he made radical changes to the nation's economic system. Favoring a more socialistic form of government, FDR implemented the New Deal. It provided welfare funds for the unemployed, promised social security for the old and disabled, and created millions of jobs in the public sector. The plan, however, was not as effective as people hoped. Not until the advent of World War II and the need for private industry to manufacture goods for the military did the economy truly improve.

World War II. The depression of the 1930s was felt worldwide. The social unrest in European countries created the opportunity for fascist leaders to rise to power. Adolf Hitler, propelled by a belief in Nietzche's "superhuman," sought to create a perfect race that would rule the world by force. Germans desiring supremacy followed his plan of attack and helped to exterminate millions of Jews. Benito Mussolini in Italy and Fransciso Franco in Spain were also fascist dictators who promised to lead their people out of economic duress by leading them into war.

World War II began in 1939 and ended in 1945. As in World War I, two coalitions engaged in combat. The conflict involved air, land, and sea battles and was the most devastating in human history. Holding to its strong isolationist sentiment, the United States was reluctant to enter the war; but on December 7, 1941, the Japanese bombed Pearl Harbor, awakening the "sleeping giant." Afterward, the United States joined the Allies — which included Great Britain, the Soviet Union, and France — and declared war on the Axis powers (Germany, Japan, and Italy). After several years of fighting, the war ended with Germany and Japan's defeat and surrender.

The Fundamentals. Religious reactions to the modern era were varied. The debate between Protestants over the adaptability of the Christian faith to modern ideas and concepts was of particular significance. The controversy was divided into two camps. The modernists argued for a faith more compliant to the advances in modern science and the changing culture. The fundamentalists, on the other hand, were unwilling to compromise the orthodox beliefs of Christianity for the sake of becoming "relevant" to a godless society. The Bible was at the heart of the controversy. The fundamentalists, consisting mainly of conservative Baptists and Presbyterians, insisted upon the inerrancy and authority of Scripture. The modernists saw the Bible as just another religious book to be used for the general good of all people. They did not believe that it was the ultimate guide to faith and life.

Many liberals characterized the fundamentalists as ignorant and legalistic because of their unwavering stand and apparent disregard for science. However, some fundamentalists argued their position in very learned circles; one example, J. Gresham Machen (1881–1937) was a professor of New Testament theology at Princeton Seminary. In his book *Christianity and Liberalism*, Machen made a powerful case for the fundamentals of the faith by pointing out several flaws in the modernist/liberal attempt to reconcile scientific theory with Christian beliefs. He left the reader no room to doubt his assertion that their beliefs were "unscientific" and "un-Christian." So thorough and logical was Machen's work, that he even won the respect of H.L. Menken, a well-known critic of Christianity's influence on America.

In the 1920s and 1930s, fundamentalism acknowledged the Bible as the remedy to society's problems. As the Word of God, it did not need to be altered. Although modernists did not want to hear it, the Bible's proclamation that God saves sinners was the message they needed to hear. Its offer of redemption and reformation was the only relevant answer to a world ripped apart by death and sin.

Modernism. In the aftermath of World War I, art began to reflect the pessimism and discontinuity of the age. The international movement in art called modernism rejected the appearance of order in favor of unrelated fragments and shapes. The artists believed this to be a true representation of the world. Reality, as they viewed it, was not neat and structured. Their works lacked the sense of resolution and harmony that had been present in the art of the previous century. The music, sculpture, painting, and literature of the time demonstrated the breakdown in the world's economic, political, and social systems. "Modernism assumed that the world had moved into a post-Christian era," noted one writer.

The Lost Generation. During the 1920s, American artists and writers sought aesthetic refuge in Paris. The expatriates thought that the American public was not appreciating their work. The group of artists hoped to enhance their abilities and thus lift American art and literature to a "higher level." Almost every writer of significance traveled to Paris in search of the artistic support that was lacking at home. F. Scott Fitzgerald, Ezra Pound, T. S. Eliot, E. E. Cummings, and Robert Frost were among the Parisian expatriates. One of the most influential expatriates was Gertrude Stein. Her apartment in Paris was a central meeting place. Of the group of writers that surrounded her, she once said, "You are all a lost generation."

Modern Prose. Ernest Hemingway lived in Paris and was a member of the "lost generation." He included Stein's statement as an epigraph in his novel, *The Sun Also Rises* (1926). Stein was one of Hemingway's mentors. She told him, "Begin over and concentrate." Hemingway's concentration brought him to create short stories and novels that reflect a writer striving to write the "truest sentence." His tight form of writing revealed an economy of words that was reflective of the modernist style to "compress emotion and narration."

Unlike the novels of the nineteenth century, which were expected to be long and directed by an authoritative narrator, modernism favored the short story with its economy of words and subjective point of view. In his novel *As I Lay Dying,* William Faulkner (not featured in this study) demonstrated the modernist technique of narration by telling the story from the point of view of each of the characters. The fragmented and dark tale is often amusing but demonstrates well the modernist concept that truth is a matter of interpretation.

Modern Poetry. "After one has abandoned a belief in God," Wallace Stevens wrote, "poetry is that essence which takes its place as life's redemption." Because of their concentrated passion, the poets of the modern era were highly influential in shaping modern literature. Modern American poetry contained elements of imagism or experimentalism, traditionalism and regionalism, all of which were later to be found in works of prose and drama.

T. S. Eliot's long poem *The Wasteland* (1922) captured the modern mood of skepticism and despair with penetrating precision. The work shows the marks of the influence of its editor, Ezra Pound. The poem contains elements of imagism. This movement that Pound started and encouraged rejected the romantic sentimentality of the nineteenth century. It used, as Pound described, "an intellectual and emotional complex in an instant of time." The intellectual aspect of the poetry was manifested in hard, concrete visual images. The emotional was the sound and rhythm of the poem. Imagism demanded the use of common language that suggested rather than completed statements.

The Harlem Renaissance. Jazz and blues were popular musical styles during the 1920s. The rhythm was rooted in the musical expression of blacks emerging from the South. Black writers from Harlem, a section of New York City, carried the beat over into various forms of literature and sought to establish a cultural center equal to that of the whites in Paris. The Harlem Renaissance started with the publication of Countee Cullen's "I Have a Rendezvous with Life (with apologies to Alan Seeger)" in 1921. Other writers and intellectuals quickly followed with works that captured the attention of the nation. Langston Hughes, Harlem's most popular poet, inspired blacks to be proud of their heritage. The concerted effort by black artists opened eyes to an America that had remained tucked away in the segregated corners of the nation.

Answer *true* or *false* for each of the following statements.

1.1   _____   The "modern temper" was uncertain and distrustful of science and religion.

1.2   _____   World War I proved that society had succeeded in bringing peace and happiness to everyone.

1.3   _____   World War I was a worldwide struggle for political, economic, and military supremacy.

1.4   _____   America was reluctant to involve itself in European affairs.

1.5   _____   The large-scale loss of life in World War I caused writers to be optimistic.

1.6   _____   After the war, Americans were content with traditional manners and beliefs.

1.7   _____   The 1930s were known as the Jazz Age.

1.8 _____ The advent of mass communication created a new culture.

1.9 _____ Popular culture helped to spread the desire for social permissiveness and the pursuit of pleasure.

1.10 _____ The automobile had little effect on American society and culture.

1.11 _____ The Eighteenth Amendment to the U.S. Constitution was largely obeyed.

1.12 _____ The Nineteenth Amendment to the U.S. Constitution gave women the right to vote.

1.13 _____ Political oppression brought occupational and educational independence for women.

1.14 _____ Sigmund Freud theorized that all of man's problems stem from satisfied desires.

1.15 _____ In October 1929, the stock market crash left millions of people jobless and hungry.

1.16 _____ By 1932, more than 25 percent of the nation's workers were unemployed.

1.17 _____ During the 1930s, communism was popular among union workers and the intellectual elite.

1.18 _____ President Franklin D. Roosevelt made no changes to the nation's economic system.

1.19 _____ In the midst of the Depression, the New Deal provided welfare funds for the unemployed, promised social security for the old and disabled, and created millions of jobs in the public sector.

1.20 _____ The depression of the 1930s was felt worldwide, creating social unrest in Europe and the opportunity for the rise of fascist leaders.

1.21 _____ World War II was the most devastating war in human history.

1.22 _____ At the heart of the Fundamentalist/Modernist controversy was the Bible.

1.23 _____ Religious Modernists argued for a faith more compliant to the advances in modern science and the changing culture.

1.24 _____ Fundamentalists denied the inerrancy and authority of Scripture.

1.25 _____ After World War I, art began to reflect the pessimism and discontinuity of the modern age.

1.26 _____ Modernism assumed that the world had moved into a post-Christian era.

1.27 _____ Almost every writer of significance traveled to London in search of the artistic support that was lacking at home.

1.28 _____ An economy of words is reflective of the modernist style of prose.

1.29 _____ The modernist style compresses emotion and narration.

1.30 _____ In the modernist movement, truth was a matter of interpretation.

1.31 _____ Modern American poetry contains elements of imagism, traditionalism, and regionalism.

1.32 _____ Modern works of prose and drama do not have elements of modern poetry.

1.33 _____ Imagism rejected the romantic sentimentality of the nineteenth century.

1.34 _____ Black writers of the Harlem Renaissance carried the rhythm of classical music over into various forms of literature.

1.35 _____ The Harlem Renaissance was an attempt by black writers to establish a cultural center equal to that of the whites in Paris.

MODERN PROSE

Ernest Hemingway (1899–1961). Ernest Hemingway is one of the most remembered writers of his time. He was known for his lifestyle as much as for his writing. He lived far from the control and influence of his Methodist roots. He wrote without the words that reminded him of "sacred" things. A tragedy of religious perfectionism, Hemingway announced somberly near the end of his life, "I live in a vacuum that is as lonely as a radio tube when the batteries are dead and there is no current to plug into."

Hemingway was born and raised in Oak Park, Illinois, a "stronghold of conservative politics and morality." His grandfather, Anson Hemingway, was a close friend of Dwight L. Moody and the general secretary of the Young Men's Christian Association (YMCA). Hemingway's maternal grandfather was also a powerful religious figure in his life. Called "Abba" by his grandchildren, Ernest Hall, led the family in prayer and Bible lessons, speaking of God and to God as if he knew Him intimately. Hemingway's own father, a successful physician, once aspired to serve as a missionary.

Despite these examples of piety, Hemingway decided to walk down another road. Disappointing his parents, he refused to attend college after high school and got a job as a reporter for the *Kansas City Star*. At the outbreak of World War I, Hemingway wanted to fight, but he was unable to serve in the United States Army because of a boxing injury to his left eye. Instead, he joined the Red Cross ambulance corps. Within three weeks of entering service in Italy, he was severely wounded by shrapnel. He spent several months recovering in a hospital in Milan. His novel *A Farewell to Arms* (1926) was based on these experiences.

Hemingway returned home a decorated hero, but his exposure to war only solidified his feelings of betrayal and disillusionment. Restless within the confines of his parents' home and beliefs, Hemingway retreated to the family cottage in northern Michigan to write, but success continued to elude him. At the age of twenty-one, he married Hadley Richardson, a wealthy older woman. The two moved to Paris to further Hemingway's career as a writer. The couple settled into the expatriate community of artists and writers, joining them in their lifestyle and attitudes. Among those who helped Hemingway hone his craft and see his works put into print were Gertrude Stein, F. Scott Fitzgerald, and Sherwood Anderson.

In 1925 he published his first book of short stories, *In Our Time*. Shortly after, he published his first novel, *The Sun Also Rises* (1926). It clearly shows his desire to "write one true sentence." The novel is about a group of American and British expatriates living in Paris. While devoid of innocence and traditional mores, they try to feed their hunger for stability and meaning by creating their own set of rules. Finally, they are still left with only disillusionment and bitterness.

As an international celebrity, Hemingway traveled the world hunting wild game and socializing in famous bars. He married four times and practiced an overindulgent lifestyle. The passing years brought only a more intense thirst for adventure and danger. During the Spanish Civil War, he became a war correspondent and became passionately involved in the conflict. His novel *For Whom the Bell Tolls* (1940) is an earnest plea for the overthrow of the fascist dictator Generalissimo Franco.

Gertrude Stein once told Hemingway to "begin over and concentrate." And he did. His writing style is clear and precise, an adaptation of his journalistic experience. He avoided adjectives and focused on the "weight" of his nouns. At times, his words can seem choppy as if you are reading a telegraph. This effect stemmed from his desire to recreate reality by forsaking ideas and words like "*sacred, glorious,* and *sacrifice.*" To him, they were just products of sentimental and weak individuals; they did not exist. Life was only bitterness and pain. He guided himself by saying, "Write the truest sentence you know."

In 1954 Hemingway was awarded the Nobel Prize for literature in recognition of his short novel (called a novella) *The Old Man and the Sea* (1952). William Faulkner described the Pulitzer Prize-winning work and the significant change in Hemingway's writing thus: "Hemingway has discovered God the Creator. Until now, his men and women had made themselves, shaped themselves out of their own clay. But this time he wrote about pity: about something somewhere that made them all and loved them all and pitied them all." Hemingway was never able truly to forget his religious upbringing.

Hemingway frequently suffered from bouts of despair. He blamed his mother for his father's suicide and refused to speak to her. During the latter part of his life, Hemingway was hospitalized several times for manic depression and paranoia. In 1961 shortly after being pronounced well, he pressed a gun to his head and destroyed himself. He never understood what it was to have peace with God.

Fill in each of the blanks using items from the following word list:

truest	ambulance	conservative
Spanish Civil War	clear	reporter
depression	hunting	socializing
Milan	nouns	adjectives
Paris		

1.36   Ernest Hemingway was born and raised in a stronghold of _____ politics and morality.

1.37   After high school, he took a job as a _____ for the *Kansas City Star*.

1.38   He joined the Red Cross _____ corps during World War I.

1.39   Hemingway spent several months in a hospital in _____ recovering from shrapnel wounds.

1.40   Hemingway moved with his wife to _____ to further his career as a writer.

1.41   An adaptation of his journalistic experience, Hemingway's writing style is _____ and precise.

1.42   Hemingway avoided _____ and focused on the weight of his

_____ .

1.43   He told himself to "write the _____ sentence you know."

1.44   As an international celebrity, Hemingway traveled the world _____

wild game and _____ in famous bars.

1.45   During the _____, he served as a war correspondent.

1.46   Hemingway frequently suffered from bouts of _____ .

What to Look For:

Hemingway's short stories are typical of modernist literature. His characters often display the confusion and frustration of modern life, and his stories often lack resolution. As you read the following selection, look for elements of modernism. Do the characters have hope? Is there a sense of honor or patriotism among the wounded? In what does the doctor encourage them to put their trust? Does the story have a definite ending?

In Another Country

IN THE FALL THE WAR WAS ALWAYS there, but we did not go to it any more. It was cold in the fall in Milan and the dark came very early. Then the electric lights came on, and it was pleasant along the streets looking in the windows. There was much game hanging outside the shops, and the snow powdered in the fur of the foxes and the wind blew their tails. The deer hung stiff and heavy and empty, and small birds blew in the wind and the wind turned their feathers. It was a cold fall and the wind came down from the mountains.

We were all at the hospital every afternoon, and there were different ways of walking across the town through the dusk to the hospital. Two of the ways were alongside canals, but they were long. Always, though, you crossed a bridge across a canal to enter the hospital. There was a choice of three bridges. On one of them a woman sold roasted chestnuts. It was warm, standing in front of her charcoal fire, and the chestnuts were warm afterward in your pocket. The hospital was very old and very beautiful, and you entered through a gate and walked across a courtyard and out a gate on the other side. There were usually funerals starting from the courtyard. Beyond the old hospital were the new brick pavilions, and there we met every afternoon and were all very polite and interested in what was the matter, and sat in the machines that were to make so much difference.

The doctor came up to the machine where I was sitting and said: "What did you like best to do before the war? Did you practice a sport?"

I said: "Yes, football."

"Good" he said. "You will be able to play football again better than ever."

My knee did not bend and the leg dropped straight from the knee to the ankle without a calf, and the machine was to bend the knee and make it move as in riding a tricycle. But it did not bend yet, and instead the machine lurched when it came to the bending part. The doctor said: "That will all pass. You are a fortunate young man. You will play football again like a champion."

In the next machine was a major who had a little hand like a baby's. He winked at me when the doctor examined his hand, which was between two leather straps that bounced up and down and flapped the stiff fingers, and said: "And will I too play football, captain-doctor?" He had been a very great fencer, and before the war the greatest fencer in Italy.

The doctor went to his office in a back room and brought a photograph which showed a hand that had been withered almost as small as the major's, before it had taken a machine course, and after was a little larger. The major held the photograph with his good hand and looked at it very carefully. "A wound?" he asked.

"An industrial accident," the doctor said.

"Very interesting, very interesting," the major said, and handed it back to the doctor.

"You have confidence?"

"No," said the major.

There were three boys who came each day who were about the same age I was. They were all three from Milan, and one of them was to be a lawyer, and one was to be a painter, and one had intended to be a soldier, and after we were finished with the machines, sometimes we walked back together to the Café Cova, which was next door to the Scala. We walked the short way through the communist quarter because we were four together. The people hated us because we were officers, and from a wineshop some one would call out, *"A basso gli ufficiali!"* as we passed. Another boy who walked with us sometimes and made us five wore a black silk handkerchief across his face because he had no nose then and his face was to be rebuilt. He had gone out to the front from the military academy and been wounded within an hour after he had gone into the front line for the first time. They rebuilt his face, but he came from a very old family and they could never get the nose exactly right. He went to South America and worked in a bank. But this was a long time ago, and then we did not any of us know how it was going to be afterward. We only knew then that there was always the war, but that we were not going to it any more.

We all had the same medals, except the boy with the black silk bandage across his face, and he had not been at the front long enough to get any medals. The tall boy with a very pale face who was to be a lawyer had been a lieutenant of *Arditi* and had three medals of the sort we each had only one of. He had lived a very long time with death and was a little detached. We were all a little detached, and there was nothing that held us together except that we met every afternoon at the hospital. Although, as we walked to the Cova through the tough part of town, walking in the dark, with light and singing coming out of the wine-shops, and sometimes having to walk into the street when the men and women would crowd together on the sidewalk so that we would have had to jostle them to get by, we felt held together by there being something that had happened that they, the people who disliked us, did not understand.

We ourselves all understood the Cova, where it was rich and warm and not too brightly lighted, and noisy and smoky at certain hours, and there were always girls at the tables and the illustrated papers on a rack on the wall. The girls at the Cova were very patriotic, and I found that the most patriotic people in Italy were the café girls—and I believe they are still patriotic.

The boys at first were very polite about my medals and asked me what I had done to get them. I showed them the papers, which were written in very beautiful language and full of *fratellanza* and *abnegazione*, but which really said, with the adjectives removed, that I had been given the medals because I was an American. After that their manner changed a little toward me, although I was their friend against outsiders. I was a friend, but I was never really one of them after they had read the citations, because it had been different with them and they had done very different things to get their medals. I had been wounded, it was true; but we all knew that being wounded, after all, was really an accident. I was never ashamed of the ribbons, though, and sometimes, after the cocktail hour, I would imagine myself having done all the things they had done to get their medals; but walking home at night through the empty streets with the cold wind and all the shops closed, trying to keep near the street lights, I knew that I would never have done such things, and I was very much afraid to die, and often lay in bed at night by myself, afraid to die and wondering how I would be when I went back to the front again.

The three with the medals were like hunting-hawks; and I was not a hawk, although I might seem a hawk to those who had never hunted; they, the three, knew better and so we drifted apart. But I stayed good friends with the boy who had been wounded his first day at the front, because he would never know now how he would have turned out; so he could never be accepted either, and I liked him because I thought perhaps he would not have turned out to be a hawk either.

The major, who had been the great fencer, did not believe in bravery, and spent much time while we sat in the machines correcting my grammar. He had complimented me on how I spoke Italian, and we talked together very easily. One day I had said that Italian seemed such an easy language to me that I could not take a great interest in it; everything was so easy to say. "Ah, yes," the major said. "Why, then, do you not take up the use of grammar?" So we took up the use of grammar, and soon Italian was such a difficult language that I was afraid to talk to him until I had the grammar straight in my mind.

The major came very regularly to the hospital. I do not think he ever missed a day, although I am sure he did not believe in the machines. There was a time when none of us believed in the machines, and one day the major said it was all nonsense. The machines were new then and it was we who were to prove them. It was an Idiotic idea, he said, "a theory, like another." I had not learned my grammar, and he said I was a stupid impossible disgrace, and he was a fool to have bothered with me. He was a small man and he sat straight up in his chair with his right hand thrust into the machine and looked straight ahead at the wall while the straps thumped up and down with his fingers in them.

"What will you do when the war is over if it is over?" he asked me.

"Speak grammatically!"

"I will go to the States."

"Are you married?"

"No, but I hope to be."

"The more of a fool you are," he said —
He seemed very angry. "A man must not marry."

"Why, Signor Maggiore?"

"Don't call me 'Signor Maggiore.'"

"Why must not a man marry?"

"He cannot marry. He cannot marry," he said angrily. "If he is to lose everything, he should not place himself in a position to lose that. He should not place himself in a position to lose. He should find things he cannot lose."

He spoke very angrily and bitterly, and looked straight ahead while he talked.

"But why should he necessarily lose it?"

"He'll lose it," the major said. He was looking at the wall. Then he looked down at the machine and jerked his little hand out from between the straps and slapped it hard against his thigh. "He'll lose it," he almost shouted. "Don't argue with me!" Then he called to the attendant who ran the machines. "Come and turn this darned thing off."

He went back into the other room for the light treatment and the massage. Then I heard him ask the doctor if he might use his telephone and he shut the door. When he came back into the room, I was sitting in another machine. He was wearing his cape and had his cap on, and he came directly toward my machine and put his arm on my shoulder.

11

"I am *so* sorry," he said, and patted me on the shoulder with his good hand. "I would not be rude. My wife has just died. You must forgive me."

"Oh—" I said, feeling sick for him. "I am *so* sorry."

He stood there biting his lower lip. "It is very difficult," he said. "I cannot resign myself."

He looked straight past me and out through the window. Then he began to cry. "I am utterly unable to resign myself," he said and choked. And then crying, his head up looking at nothing, carrying himself straight and soldierly, with tears on both his cheeks and biting his lips, he walked past the machines and out the door.

The doctor told me that the major's wife, who was very young and whom he had not married until he was definitely invalided out of the war, had died of pneumonia. She had been sick only a few days. No one expected her to die. The major did not come to the hospital for three days. Then he came at the usual hour, wearing a black band on the sleeve of his uniform. When he came back, there were large framed photographs around the wall, of all sorts of wounds before and after they had been cured by the machines. In front of the machine the major used were three photographs of hands like his that were completely restored. I do not know where the doctor got them. I always understood we were the first to use the machines. The photographs did not make much difference to the major because he only looked out of the window.

⇨ **Answer** *true* **or** *false* **for each of the following statements.**

1.47 _____ The narrator goes to the hospital every afternoon.

1.48 _____ At the hospital, patients are hooked up to machines to heal their wounds.

1.49 _____ The narrator says that he received his medals because he was a brave soldier.

1.50 _____ After reading the narrator's papers for his medals, the boys treat him with great honor.

1.51 _____ The major advises the narrator to get married.

1.52 _____ The narrator's wife dies.

1.53 _____ The major waited to marry his wife until he was out of the war.

1.54 _____ When the major returns, photographs of wounds that had been cured by the machines hang on the wall.

1.55 _____ The narrator doubts the photographs because he was one of the first patients to use the machines.

1.56 _____ Hopeful of full recovery, the major stares at the photographs of the cured hands.

1.57 _____ At the end of the story, both the narrator and the major are confident that life has meaning.

F. Scott Fitzgerald (1896–1940). The 1920s were a time of reckless desire and lasting dissatisfaction. F. Scott Fitzgerald knew the period all too well. He wrote about it, observed it, and lived it. His novels are filled with glamorous people and material acquisition. But like society, his characters are troubled by an emptiness that they cannot fill.

Fitzgerald was born and raised in St. Paul, Minnesota. He was named after a famous relative, his full name being Francis Scott Key Fitzgerald. His father was a businessman who did not attain much success. His mother was from a Southern family of wealth and importance. Although his father could provide no more than a middle-class living, the Fitzgeralds desired the company and status of people far above their means.

Fitzgerald's Briefcase

Fitzgerald was sent to a private boarding school in New Jersey and later attended Princeton University in 1913. Although he was successful in literary and dramatic activities, he never graduated. In 1917, he joined the Army and was stationed in Montgomery, Alabama, where he met and fell in love with a Southern belle named Zelda Sayre. She would not marry him unless he could provide her with the high standard of living to which she was accustomed. Fitzgerald left the Army and returned home to win her. He reworked a novel, *This Side of Paradise,* that he had begun in college and published it in 1920. The novel was an instant best seller, making Fitzgerald rich. Zelda married him a week after the book hit the stores.

Scott and Zelda spent their days and nights among the rich and glamorous. They lived in New York City and Europe, entertaining and being entertained. It was an endless pursuit of pleasure that quickly diminished Fitzgerald's earnings and health.

However, Fitzgerald continued to write. In 1921 Fitzgerald published *Flappers and Philosophers*. The collection of short stories was followed by another in 1922, *Tales of the Jazz Age*. His novel *The Beautiful and the Damned* was also published in 1922. In 1926 he wrote his most popular novel, *The Great Gatsby*. It is the story of a self-made man who abandons a strong work ethic to find fulfillment in wealth and social status. His misguided pursuits, lead him to disillusionment and death. Fitzgerald himself had become disheartened by the high-class society of which he had for so long wished to be a part.

The Great Depression of the 1930s brought change to not only the country but also those who had drunk deeply from the wells of avarice and wanton pleasure. The Fitzgeralds were no different. Zelda suffered several nervous breakdowns and was placed in a mental institution in 1930, where she stayed until the end of her life in 1947. In 1937 Scott, an alcoholic with financial difficulties, moved to Hollywood to pursue a career in screenwriting. With his earnings, he paid his debts and Zelda's medical bills.

Frustrated and unappreciated by Hollywood film-makers, he turned again to writing fiction. He wrote many more short stories and another novel, *Tender is the Night* (1934). He began another novel, *The Last Tycoon*, a story about a film mogul, but he never finished it. Fitzgerald died of a heart attack at the age of forty-four.

Fill in each of the blanks using items from the following word list.

pleasure	emptiness	Army	finished
Zelda's	Hollywood	mental	screenwriting

1.58   Fitzgerald's characters are troubled by an _____ that they cannot fill.

1.59   Fitzgerald fell in love while stationed at an _____ base in Montgomery, Alabama.

1.60   Fitzgerald wrote *This Side of Paradise* to win _____ hand in marriage.

1.61   The couple's endless pursuit of _____ quickly diminished Fitzgerald's earnings and health.

1.62   In 1930 Zelda was placed in a _____ institution, where she stayed until the end of her life.

1.63   In 1937 Fitzgerald moved to _____ to pursue a career in _____ .

1.64   His final novel, *The Last Tycoon,* was never _____ .

What to Look For:

Fitzgerald's characters are often troubled by an emptiness that they cannot fill. Their pursuit of material wealth and sensuality leaves them disillusioned and wanting something more. Before you read the following story by Fitzgerald, read and reflect upon Proverbs 5 and 7. As you read, think of the ways in which Dexter could have avoided trouble. Although Dexter does not die physically, in what ways is he willfully led "to the chambers of death?"

Winter Dreams

Some of the caddies were poor as sin and lived in one-room houses with a neurasthenic cow in the front yard, but Dexter Green's father owned the second best grocery-store in Black Bear — the best one was "The Hub," patronized by the people from Sherry Island — and Dexter caddied only for pocket-money.

In the fall when the days became crisp and gray, and the long Minnesota winter shut down like the white lid of a box, Dexter's skis moved over the snow that hid the fairways of the golf course. At these times the country gave him a feeling of profound melancholy — it offended him that the links should lie in enforced fallowness, haunted by ragged sparrows for the long season. It was dreary, too, that on the tees where the gay colors fluttered in summer there were now only the desolate sand-boxes knee-deep in crusted ice. When he crossed the hills the wind blew cold as misery, and if the sun was out he tramped with his eyes squinted up against the hard dimensionless glare.

In April the winter ceased abruptly. The snow ran down into Black Bear Lake scarcely tarrying for the early golfers to brave the season with red and black balls. Without elation, without an interval of moist glory, the cold was gone.

Dexter knew that there was something dismal about this Northern spring, just as he knew there was something gorgeous about the fall. Fall made him clinch his hands and tremble and repeat idiotic sentences to himself, and make brisk abrupt gestures of command to imaginary audiences and armies. October filled him with hope which November raised to a sort of ecstatic triumph, and in this mood the fleeting brilliant impressions of the summer at Sherry Island were ready grist to his mill. He became a golf champion and defeated Mr. T. A. Hedrick in a marvellous match played a hundred times over the fairways of his imagination, a match each detail of which he changed about untiringly — sometimes he won with almost laughable ease, sometimes he came up magnificently from behind. Again, stepping from a Pierce-Arrow automobile, like Mr. Mortimer Jones, he strolled frigidly into the lounge of the Sherry Island Golf Club — or perhaps, surrounded by an admiring crowd, he gave an exhibition of fancy diving from the spring-board of the club raft....Among those who watched him in open-mouthed wonder was Mr. Mortimer Jones.

And one day it came to pass that Mr. Jones—himself and not his ghost—came up to Dexter with tears in his eyes and said that Dexter was the — best caddy in the club, and wouldn't he decide not to quit if Mr. Jones made it worth his while, because every other caddy in the club lost one ball a hole for him — regularly —

"No, sir," said Dexter decisively, "I don't want to caddy any more." Then, after a pause: "I'm too old."

"You're not more than fourteen. Why the devil did you decide just this morning that you wanted to quit? You promised that next week you'd go over to the State tournament with me."

"I decided I was too old."

Dexter handed in his "A Class" badge, collected what money was due him from the caddy master, and walked home to Black Bear Village.

"The best — caddy I ever saw," shouted Mr. Mortimer Jones over a drink that afternoon. "Never lost a ball! Willing! Intelligent! Quiet! Honest! Grateful!"

The little girl who had done this was eleven — beautifully ugly as little girls are apt to be who are destined after a few years to be inexpressibly lovely and bring no end of misery to a great number of men. The spark, however, was perceptible. There was a general ungodliness in the way her lips twisted, down at the corners when she smiled, and in the — Heaven help us! — in the almost passionate quality of her eyes. Vitality is born early in such women. It was utterly in evidence now, shining through her thin frame in a sort of glow.

She had come eagerly out on to the course at nine o'clock with a white linen nurse and five small new golf-clubs in a white canvas bag which the nurse was carrying. When Dexter first saw her she was standing by the caddy house, rather ill at ease and trying to conceal the fact by engaging her nurse in an obviously unnatural conversation graced by startling and irrelevant grimaces from herself.

"Well, it's certainly a nice day, Hilda," Dexter heard her say. She drew down the corners of her mouth, smiled, and glanced furtively around, her eyes in transit falling for an instant on Dexter.

Then to the nurse:

"Well, I guess there aren't very many people out here this morning, are there?"

The smile again — radiant, blatantly artificial — convincing.

"I don't know what we're supposed to do now," said the nurse, looking nowhere in particular.

"Oh, that's all right. I'll fix it up."

Dexter stood perfectly still, his mouth slightly ajar. He knew that if he moved forward a step his stare would be in her line of vision — if he moved backward he would lose his full view of her face. For a moment he had not realized how young she was. Now he remembered having seen her several times the year before in bloomers.

Suddenly, involuntarily, he laughed, a short abrupt laugh — then, startled by himself, he turned and began to walk quickly away.

"Boy!"

Dexter stopped.

"Boy——"

Beyond question he was addressed. Not only that, but he was treated to that absurd smile, that preposterous smile — the memory of which at least a dozen men were to carry into middle age.

"Boy, do you know where the golf teacher is?"

"He's giving a lesson."

"Well, do you know where the caddy-master is?"

"He isn't here yet this morning."

"Oh." For a moment this baffled her. She stood alternately on her right and left foot.

"We'd like to get a caddy," said the nurse. "Mrs. Mortimer Jones sent us out to play golf, and we don't know how without we get a caddy."

Here she was stopped by an ominous glance from Miss Jones, followed immediately by the smile.

"There aren't any caddies here except me," said Dexter to the nurse, "and I got to stay here in charge until the caddy-master gets here."

"Oh."

Miss Jones and her retinue now withdrew, and at a proper distance from Dexter became involved in a heated conversation, which was concluded by Miss Jones taking one of the clubs and hitting it on the ground with violence. For further emphasis she raised it again and was about to bring it down smartly upon the nurse's bosom, when the nurse seized the club and twisted it from her hands.

"You darn little mean old thing!" cried Miss Jones wildly.

Another argument ensued. Realizing that the elements of the comedy were implied in the scene, Dexter several times began to laugh, but each time restrained the laugh before it reached audibility. He could not resist the monstrous conviction that the little girl was justified in beating the nurse.

The situation was resolved by the fortuitous appearance of the caddymaster, who was appealed to immediately by the nurse.

"Miss Jones is to have a little caddy, and this one says he can't go."

"Mr. McKenna said I was to wait here till you came," said Dexter quickly.

"Well, he's here now." Miss Jones smiled cheerfully at the caddy-master. Then she dropped her bag and set off at a haughty mince toward the first tee.

"Well?" The caddy-master turned to Dexter. "What you standing there like a dummy for? Go pick up the young lady's clubs."

"I don't think I'll go out to-day," said Dexter.

"You don't——"

"I think I'll quit."

The enormity of his decision frightened him. He was a favorite caddy, and the thirty dollars a month he earned through the summer were not to be made elsewhere around the lake. But he had received a strong emotional shock, and his perturbation required a violent and immediate outlet.

It is not so simple as that, either. As so frequently would be the case in the future, Dexter was unconsciously dictated to by his winter dreams.

II

NOW, OF COURSE, the quality and the seasonability of these winter dreams varied, but the stuff of them remained. They persuaded Dexter several years later to pass up a business course at the State university—his father, prospering now, would have paid his way—for the precarious advantage of attending an older and more famous university in the East, where he was bothered by his scanty funds. But do not get the impression, because his winter dreams happened to be concerned at first with musings on the rich, that there was anything merely snobbish in the boy. He wanted not association with glittering things and glittering people—he wanted the glittering things themselves. Often he reached out for the best without knowing why he wanted it—and sometimes he ran up against the mysterious denials and prohibitions in which life indulges. It is with one of those denials and not with his career as a whole that this story deals.

He made money. It was rather amazing. After college he went to the city from which Black Bear Lake draws its wealthy patrons. When he was only twenty-three and had been there not quite two years, there were already people who liked to say: "Now there's a boy—" All about him rich men's sons were peddling bonds precariously, or investing patrimonies precariously, or plodding through the two dozen volumes of the "George Washington Commercial Course," but Dexter borrowed a thousand dollars on his college degree and his confident mouth, and bought a partnership in a laundry.

It was a small laundry when he went into it but Dexter made a specialty of learning how the English washed fine woolen golf-stockings without shrinking them, and within a year he was catering to the trade that wore knickerbockers. Men were insisting that their Shetland hose and sweaters go to his laundry just as they had insisted on a caddy who could find golfballs. A little later he was doing their wives' lingerie as well—and running five branches in different parts of the city. Before he was twenty-seven he owned the largest string of laundries in his section of the country. It was then that he sold out and went to New York. But the part of his story that concerns us goes back to the days when he was making his first big success.

When he was twenty-three Mr. Hart—one of the gray-haired men who like to say "Now there's a boy"—gave him a guest card to the Sherry Island Golf Club for a week-end. So he signed his name one day on the register, and that afternoon played golf in a foursome with Mr. Hart and Mr. Sandwood and Mr. T. A. Hedrick. He did not consider it necessary to remark that he had once carried Mr. Hart's bag over this same links, and that he knew every trap and gully with his eyes shut—but he found himself glancing at the four caddies who trailed them, trying to catch a gleam or gesture that would remind him of himself, that would lessen the gap which lay between his present and his past.

It was a curious day, slashed abruptly with fleeting, familiar impressions. One minute he had the sense of being a trespasser—in the next he was impressed by the tremendous superiority he felt toward Mr. T. A. Hedrick, who was a bore and not even a good golfer any more.

Then, because of a ball Mr. Hart lost near the fifteenth green, an enormous thing happened. While they were searching the stiff grasses of the rough there was a clear call of "Fore!" from behind a hill in their rear. And as they all turned abruptly from their search a bright new ball sliced abruptly over the hill and caught Mr. T. A. Hedrick in the abdomen.

"By Gad!" cried Mr. T. A. Hedrick, "they ought to put some of these crazy women off the course. It's getting to be outrageous."

A head and a voice came up together over the hill:

"Do you mind if we go through?"

"You hit me in the stomach!" declared Mr. Hedrick wildly.

"Did I?" The girl approached the group of men. "I'm sorry. I yelled 'Fore!'"

Her glance fell casually on each of the men — then scanned the fairway for her ball.

"Did I bounce into the rough?"

It was impossible to determine whether this question was ingenuous or malicious. In a moment, however, she left no doubt, for as her partner came up over the hill she called cheerfully:

"Here I am! I'd have gone on the green except that I hit something."

As she took her stance for a short mashie shot, Dexter looked at her closely. She wore a blue gingham dress, rimmed at throat and shoulders with a white edging that accentuated her tan. The quality of exaggeration, of thinness, which had made her passionate eyes and down-turning mouth absurd at eleven, was gone now. She was arrestingly beautiful. The color in her cheeks was centered like the color in a picture — it was not a "high" color, but a sort of fluctuating and feverish warmth, so shaded that it seemed at any moment it would recede and disappear. This color and the mobility of her mouth gave a continual impression of flux, of intense life, of passionate vitality — balanced only partially by the sad luxury of her eyes.

She swung her mashie impatiently and without interest, pitching the ball into a sand-pit on the other side of the green. With a quick, insincere smile and a careless "Thank you!" she went on after it.

"That Judy Jones!" remarked Mr. Hedrick on the next tee, as they waited — some moments — for her to play on ahead. "All she needs is to be turned up and spanked for six months and then to be married off to an old-fashioned cavalry captain."

"My gosh, she's good-looking!" said Mr. Sandwood, who was just over thirty.

"Good-looking!" cried Mr. Hedrick contemptuously, "she always looks as if she wanted to be kissed! Turning those big cow-eyes on every calf in town!"

It was doubtful if Mr. Hedrick intended a reference to the maternal instinct.

"She'd play pretty good golf if she'd try," said Mr. Sandwood.

"She has no form," said Mr. Hedrick solemnly.

"She has a nice figure," said Mr. Sandwood.

"Better thank the Lord she doesn't drive a swifter ball," said Mr. Hart, winking at Dexter.

Later in the afternoon the sun went down with a riotous swirl of gold and varying blues and scarlets, and left the dry, rustling night of Western summer. Dexter watched from the veranda of the Golf Club, watched the even overlap of the waters in the little wind, silver molasses under the harvest-moon. Then the moon held a finger to her lips and the lake became a clear pool, pale and quiet. Dexter put on his bathing-suit and swam out to the farthest raft, where he stretched dripping on the wet canvas of the springboard.

18

There was a fish jumping and a star shining and the lights around the lake were gleaming. Over on a dark peninsula a piano was playing the songs of last summer and of summers before that — songs from "Chin-Chin" and "The Count of Luxemburg" and "The Chocolate Soldier" — and because the sound of a piano over a stretch of water had always seemed beautiful to Dexter he lay perfectly quiet and listened.

The tune the piano was playing at that moment had been gay and new five years before when Dexter was a sophomore at college. They had played it at a prom once when he could not afford the luxury of proms, and he had stood outside the gymnasium and listened. The sound of the tune precipitated in him a sort of ecstasy and it was with that ecstasy he viewed what happened to him now. It was a mood of intense appreciation, a sense that, for once, he was magnificently attune to life and that everything about him was radiating a brightness and a glamour he might never know again.

A low, pale oblong detached itself suddenly from the darkness of the island, spitting forth the reverberate sound of a racing motor-boat. Two white streamers of cleft water rolled themselves out behind it and almost immediately the boat was beside him, drowning out the hot tinkle of the piano in the drone of its spray. Dexter raising himself on his arms was aware of a figure standing at the wheel, of two dark eyes regarding him over the lengthening space of water — then the boat had gone by and was sweeping in an immense and purposeless circle of spray round and round in the middle of the lake. With equal eccentricity one of the circles flattened out and headed back toward the raft.

"Who's that?" she called, shutting off her motor. She was so near now that Dexter could see her bathing-suit, which consisted apparently of pink rompers.

The nose of the boat bumped the raft, and as the latter tilted rakishly he was precipitated toward her. With different degrees of interest they recognized each other.

"Aren't you one of those men we played through this afternoon?" she demanded.

He was.

"Well, do you know how to drive a motor-boat? Because if you do I wish you'd drive this one so I can ride on the surf-board behind. My name is Judy Jones" — she favored him with an absurd smirk — rather, what tried to be a smirk, for, twist her mouth as she might, it was not grotesque, it was merely beautiful — "and I live in a house over there on the island, and in that house there is a man waiting for me. When he drove up at the door I drove out of the dock because he says I'm his ideal."

There was a fish jumping and a star shining and the lights around the lake were gleaming. Dexter sat beside Judy Jones and she explained how her boat was driven. Then she was in the water, swimming to the floating surfboard with a sinuous crawl. Watching her was without effort to the eye, watching a branch waving or a sea-gull flying. Her arms, burned to butternut, moved sinuously among the dull platinum ripples, elbow appearing first, casting the forearm back with a cadence of falling water, then reaching out and down, stabbing a path ahead.

They moved out into the lake; turning, Dexter saw that she was kneeling on the low rear of the now uptilted surf-board.

"Go faster," she called, "fast as it'll go."

Obediently he jammed the lever forward and the white spray mounted at the bow. When he looked around again the girl was standing up on the rushing board, her arms spread wide, her eyes lifted toward the moon.

19

"It's awful cold," she shouted. "What's your name?"

He told her.

"Well, why don't you come to dinner to-morrow night?"

His heart turned over like the fly-wheel of the boat, and, for the second time, her casual whim gave a new direction to his life.

III

NEXT EVENING while he waited for her to come down-stairs, Dexter peopled the soft deep summer room and the sun-porch that opened from it with the men who had already loved Judy Jones. He knew the sort of men they were—the men who when he first went to college had entered from the great prep schools with graceful clothes and the deep tan of healthy summers. He had seen that, in one sense, he was better than these men. He was newer and stronger. Yet in acknowledging to himself that he wished his children to be like them he was admitting that he was but the rough, strong stuff from which they eternally sprang.

When the time had come for him to wear good clothes, he had known who were the best tailors in America, and the best tailors in America had made him the suit he wore this evening. He had acquired that particular reserve peculiar to his university, that set it off from other universities. He recognized the value to him of such a mannerism and he had adopted it; he knew that to be careless in dress and manner required more confidence than to be careful. But carelessness was for his children. His mother's name had been Krimslich. She was a Bohemian of the peasant class and she had talked broken English to the end of her days. Her son must keep to the set patterns.

At a little after seven Judy Jones came down-stairs. She wore a blue silk afternoon dress, and he was disappointed at first that she had not put on something more elaborate. This feeling was accentuated when, after a brief greeting, she went to the door of a butler's pantry and pushing it open called: "You can serve dinner, Martha." He had rather expected that a butler would announce dinner, that there would be a cocktail. Then he put these thoughts behind him as they sat down side by side on a lounge and looked at each other.

"Father and mother won't be here," she said thoughtfully.

He remembered the last time he had seen her father, and he was glad the parents were not to be here to-night—they might wonder who he was. He had been born in Keeble, a Minnesota village fifty miles farther north, and he always gave Keeble as his home instead of Black Bear Village. Country towns were well enough to come from if they weren't inconveniently in sight and used as footstools by fashionable lakes.

They talked of his university, which she had visited frequently during the past two years, and of the near-by city which supplied Sherry Island with its patrons, and whither Dexter would return next day to his prospering laundries.

During dinner she slipped into a moody depression which gave Dexter a feeling of uneasiness. Whatever petulance she uttered in her throaty voice worried him. Whatever she smiled at — at him, at a chicken liver, at nothing — it disturbed him that her smile could have no root in mirth, or even in amusement. When the scarlet corners of her lips curved down, it was less a smile than an invitation to a kiss.

Then, after dinner, she led him out on the dark sun-porch and deliberately changed the atmosphere.

"Do you mind if I weep a little?" she said.

"I'm afraid I'm boring you," he responded quickly.

"You're not. I like you. But I've just had a terrible afternoon. There was a man I cared about, and this afternoon he told me out of a clear sky that he was poor as a churchmouse. He'd never even hinted it before. Does this sound horribly mundane?"

"Perhaps he was afraid to tell you."

"Suppose he was," she answered. "He didn't start right. You see, if I'd thought of him as poor — well, I've been mad about loads of poor men, and fully intended to marry them all. But in this case, I hadn't thought of him that way, and my interest in him wasn't strong enough to survive the shock. As if a girl calmly informed her fiancee that she was a widow. He might not object to widows, but ——

"Let's start right," she interrupted herself suddenly. "Who are you, anyhow?"

For a moment Dexter hesitated. Then:

"I'm nobody," he announced. "My career is largely a matter of futures."

"Are you poor?"

"No," he said frankly, "I'm probably making more money than any man my age in the Northwest. I know that's an obnoxious remark, but you advised me to start right."

There was a pause. Then she smiled and the corners of her mouth drooped and an almost imperceptible sway brought her closer to him, looking up into his eyes. A lump rose in Dexter's throat, and he waited breathless for the experiment, facing the unpredictable compound that would form mysteriously from the elements of their lips. Then he saw—she communicated her excitement to him, lavishly, deeply, with kisses that were not a promise but a fulfillment. They aroused in him not hunger demanding renewal but surfeit that would demand more surfeit...kisses that were like charity, creating want by holding back nothing at all.

It did not take him many hours to decide that he had wanted Judy Jones ever since he was a proud, desirous little boy.

IV

IT BEGAN like that—and continued, with varying shades of intensity, on such a note right up to the dénouement. Dexter surrendered a part of himself to the most direct and unprincipled personality with which he had ever come in contact. Whatever Judy wanted, she went after with the full pressure of her charm. There was no divergence of method, no jockeying for position or premeditation of effects—there was a very little mental side to any of her affairs. She simply made men conscious to the highest degree of her physical loveliness. Dexter had no desire to change her. Her deficiencies were knit up with a passionate energy that transcended and justified them.

When, as Judy's head lay against his shoulder that first night, she whispered, "I don't know what's the matter with me. Last night I thought I was in love with a man and to-night I think I'm in love with you ——" — it seemed to him a beautiful and romantic thing to say. It was the exquisite excitability that for the moment he

21

controlled and owned. But a week later he was compelled to view this same quality in a different light. She took him in her roadster to a picnic supper, and after supper she disappeared, likewise in her roadster, with another man. Dexter became enormously upset and was scarcely able to be decently civil to the other people present. When she assured him that she had not kissed the other man, he knew she was lying — yet he was glad that she had taken the trouble to lie to him.

He was, as he found before the summer ended, one of a varying dozen who circulated about her. Each of them had at one time been favored above all others — about half of them still basked in the solace of occasional sentimental revivals. Whenever one showed signs of dropping out through long neglect, she granted him a brief honeyed hour, which encouraged him to tag along for a year or so longer. Judy made these forays upon the helpless and defeated without malice, indeed half unconscious that there was anything mischievous in what she did.

When a new man came to town every one dropped out — dates were automatically cancelled.

The helpless part of trying to do anything about it was that she did it all herself. She was not a girl who could be "won" in the kinetic sense—she was proof against cleverness, she was proof against charm; if any of these assailed her too strongly she would immediately resolve the affair to a physical basis, and under the magic of her physical splendor the strong as well as the brilliant played her game and not their own. She was entertained only by the gratification of her desires and by the direct exercise of her own charm. Perhaps from so much youthful love, so many youthful lovers, she had come, in self-defense, to nourish herself wholly from within.

Succeeding Dexter's first exhilaration came restlessness and dissatisfaction. The helpless ecstasy of losing himself in her was opiate rather than tonic. It was fortunate for his work during the winter that those moments of ecstasy came infrequently. Early in their acquaintance it had seemed for a while that there was a deep and spontaneous mutual attraction that first August, for example — three days of long evenings on her dusky veranda, of strange wan kisses through the late afternoon, in shadowy alcoves or behind the protecting trellises of the garden arbors, of mornings when she was fresh as a dream and almost shy at meeting him in the clarity of the rising day. There was all the ecstasy of an engagement about it, sharpened by his realization that there was no engagement. It was during those three days that, for the first time, he had asked her to marry him. She said "maybe some day," she said "kiss me," she said "I'd like to marry you," she said "I love you" — she said — nothing.

The three days were interrupted by the arrival of a New York man who visited at her house for half September. To Dexter's agony, rumor engaged them. The man was the son of the president of a great trust company. But at the end of a month it was reported that Judy was yawning. At a dance one night she sat all evening in a motor-boat with a local beau, while the New Yorker searched the club for her frantically. She told the local beau that she was bored with her visitor, and two days later he left. She was seen with him at the station, and it was reported that he looked very mournful indeed.

On this note the summer ended. Dexter was twenty-four, and he found himself increasingly in a position to do as he wished. He joined two clubs in the city and lived at one of them. Though he was by no means an integral part of the stag-lines at these clubs, he managed to be on hand at dances where Judy Jones was likely to appear. He could have gone out socially as much as he liked — he was an eligible young man, now, and popular with down-town fathers. His confessed devotion to Judy Jones had rather solidified his position. But he had no social aspirations and rather despised the dancing men who were always on tap for the Thursday or Saturday parties and who filled in at dinners with the younger married set. Already he was playing with the idea of going East to New York. He wanted to take Judy Jones with him. No disillusion as to the world in which she had grown up could cure his illusion as to her desirability.

Remember that—for only in the light of it can what he did for her be understood.

Eighteen months after he first met Judy Jones he became engaged to another girl. Her name was Irene Scheerer, and her father was one of the men who had always believed in Dexter. Irene was light-haired and sweet and honorable, and a little stout, and she had two suitors whom she pleasantly relinquished when Dexter formally asked her to marry him.

Summer, fall, winter, spring, another summer, another fall — so much he had given of his active life to the incorrigible lips of Judy Jones. She had treated him with interest, with encouragement, with malice, with indifference, with contempt. She had inflicted on him the innumerable little slights and indignities possible in such a case — as if in revenge for having ever cared for him at all. She had beckoned him and yawned at him and beckoned him again and he had responded often with bitterness and narrowed eyes. She had brought him ecstatic happiness and intolerable agony of spirit. She had caused him untold inconvenience and not a little trouble. She had insulted him, and she had ridden over him, and she had played his interest in her against his interest in his work — for fun. She had done everything to him except to criticize him — this she had not done — it seemed to him only because it might have sullied the utter indifference she manifested and sincerely felt toward him.

When autumn had come and gone again it occurred to him that he could not have Judy Jones. He had to beat this into his mind but he convinced himself at last. He lay awake at night for a while and argued it over. He told himself the trouble and the pain she had caused him, he enumerated her glaring deficiencies as a wife. Then he said to himself that he loved her, and after a while he fell asleep. For a week, lest he imagined her husky voice over the telephone or her eyes opposite him at lunch, he worked hard and late, and at night he went to his office and plotted out his years.

At the end of a week he went to a dance and cut in on her once. For almost the first time since they had met he did not ask her to sit out with him or tell her that she was lovely. It hurt him that she did not miss these things — that was all. He was not jealous when he saw that there was a new man tonight. He had been hardened against jealousy long before.

He stayed late at the dance. He sat for an hour with Irene Scheerer and talked about books and about music. He knew very little about either. But he was beginning to be master of his own time now, and he had a rather priggish notion that he — the young and already fabulously successful Dexter Green — should know more about such things.

That was in October, when he was twenty-five. In January, Dexter and Irene became engaged. It was to be announced in June, and they were to be married three months later.

The Minnesota winter prolonged itself interminably, and it was almost May when the winds came soft and the snow ran down into Black Bear Lake at last. For the first time in over a year Dexter was enjoying a certain tranquility of spirit. Judy Jones had been in Florida, and afterward in Hot Springs, and somewhere she had been engaged, and somewhere she had broken it off. At first, when Dexter had definitely given her up, it had made him sad that people still linked them together and asked for news of her, but when he began to be placed at dinner next to Irene Scheerer people didn't ask him about her any more — they told him about her. He ceased to be an authority on her.

May at last. Dexter walked the streets at night when the darkness was damp as rain, wondering that so soon, with so little done, so much of ecstasy had gone from him. May one year back had been marked by Judy's poignant, unforgivable, yet forgiven turbulence — it had been one of those rare times when he fancied she had grown to care for him. That old penny's worth of happiness he had spent for this bushel of content. He knew that Irene would be no more than a curtain spread behind him, a hand moving among gleaming tea-cups, a voice calling to children... fire and loveliness were gone, the magic of nights and the wonder of the varying hours and seasons...slender lips, down-turning, dropping to his lips and bearing him up into a heaven of eyes... The thing was deep in him. He was too strong and alive for it to die lightly.

In the middle of May when the weather balanced for a few days on the thin bridge that led to deep summer he turned in one night at Irene's house. Their engagement was to be announced in a week now — no one would be surprised at it. And to-night they would sit together on the lounge at the University Club and look on for an hour at the dancers. It gave him a sense of solidity to go with her — she was so sturdily popular, so intensely "great."

He mounted the steps of the brownstone house and stepped inside.

"Irene," he called.

Mrs. Scheerer came out of the living-room to meet him.

"Dexter," she said, "Irene's gone up-stairs with a splitting headache. She wanted to go with you but I made her go to bed."

"Nothing serious, I —— "

"Oh, no. She's going to play golf with you in the morning. You can spare her for just one night, can't you, Dexter?"

Her smile was kind. She and Dexter liked each other. In the living-room he talked for a moment before he said good-night.

Returning to the University Club, where he had rooms, he stood in the doorway for a moment and watched the dancers. He leaned against the door-post, nodded at a man or two — yawned.

"Hello, darling."

The familiar voice at his elbow startled him. Judy Jones had left a man and crossed the room to him — Judy Jones, a slender enamelled doll in cloth of gold: gold in a band at her head, gold in two slipper points at her dress's hem. The fragile glow of her face seemed to blossom as she smiled at him. A breeze of warmth and light blew through the room. His hands in the pockets of his dinner-jacket tightened spasmodically. He was filled with a sudden excitement.

"When did you get back?" he asked casually.

"Come here and I'll tell you about it."

She turned and he followed her. She had been away — he could have wept at the wonder of her return. She had passed through enchanted streets, doing things that were like provocative music. All mysterious happenings, all fresh and quickening hopes, had gone away with her, come back with her now.

She turned in the doorway.

"Have you a car here? If you haven't, I have."

"I have a coupé."

In then, with a rustle of golden cloth. He slammed the door. Into so many cars she had stepped — like this — like that — her back against the leather, so — her elbow resting on the door — waiting. She would have been soiled long since had there been anything to soil her — except herself — but this was her own self out-pouring.

With an effort he forced himself to start the car and back into the street. This was nothing, he must remember. She had done this before, and he had put her behind him, as he would have crossed a bad account from his books.

He drove slowly down-town and, affecting abstraction, traversed the deserted streets of the business section, peopled here and there where a movie was giving out its crowd or where consumptive or pugilistic youth lounged in front of pool halls. The clink of glasses and the slap of hands on the bars issued from saloons, cloisters of glazed glass and dirty yellow light.

She was watching him closely and the silence was embarrassing, yet in this crisis he could find no casual word with which to profane the hour. At a convenient turning he began to zigzag back toward the University Club.

"Have you missed me?" she asked suddenly.

"Everybody missed you."

He wondered if she knew of Irene Scheerer. She had been back only a day — her absence had been almost contemporaneous with his engagement.

"What a remark!" Judy laughed sadly — without sadness. She looked at him searchingly. He became absorbed in the dashboard.

"You're handsomer than you used to be," she said thoughtfully. "Dexter, you have the most rememberable eyes."

He could have laughed at this, but he did not laugh. It was the sort of thing that was said to sophomores. Yet it stabbed at him.

"I'm awfully tired of everything, darling." She called every one darling, endow-ing the endearment with careless, individual comraderie. "I wish you'd marry me."

The directness of this confused him. He should have told her now that he was going to marry another girl, but he could not tell her. He could as easily have sworn that he had never loved her.

"I think we'd get along," she continued, on the same note, "unless probably you've forgotten me and fallen in love with another girl."

Her confidence was obviously enormous. She had said, in effect, that she found such a thing impossible to believe, that if it were true he had merely committed a childish indiscretion—and probably to show off. She would forgive him, because it was not a matter of any moment but rather something to be brushed aside lightly.

"Of course you could never love anybody but me," she continued. "I like the way you love me. Oh, Dexter, have you forgotten last year?"

"No, I haven't forgotten."

"Neither have I! "

Was she sincerely moved — or was she carried along by the wave of her own acting?

25

"I wish we could be like that again," she said, and he forced himself to answer:

"I don't think we can."

"I suppose not...I hear you're giving Irene Scheerer a violent rush."

There was not the faintest emphasis on the name, yet Dexter was suddenly ashamed.

"Oh, take me home," cried Judy suddenly; "I don't want to go back to that idiotic dance — with those children."

Then, as he turned up the street that led to the residence district, Judy began to cry quietly to herself. He had never seen her cry before.

The dark street lightened, the dwellings of the rich loomed up around them, he stopped his coupé in front of the great white bulk of the Mortimer Joneses house, somnolent, gorgeous, drenched with the splendor of the damp moonlight. Its solidity startled him. The strong walls, the steel of the girders, the breadth and beam and pomp of it were there only to bring out the contrast with the young beauty beside him. It was sturdy to accentuate her slightness — as if to show what a breeze could be generated by a butterfly's wing.

He sat perfectly quiet, his nerves in wild clamor, afraid that if he moved he would find her irresistibly in his arms. Two tears had rolled down her wet face and trembled on her upper lip.

"I'm more beautiful than anybody else," she said brokenly, "why can't I be happy?" Her moist eyes tore at his stability — her mouth turned slowly downward with an exquisite sadness: "I'd like to marry you if you'll have me, Dexter. I suppose you think I'm not worth having, but I'll be so beautiful for you, Dexter."

A million phrases of anger, pride, passion, hatred, tenderness fought on his lips. Then a perfect wave of emotion washed over him, carrying off with it a sediment of wisdom, of convention, of doubt, of honor. This was his girl who was speaking, his own, his beautiful, his pride.

"Won't you come in?" He heard her draw in her breath sharply.

Waiting.

"All right," his voice was trembling, "I'll come in.

V

IT WAS STRANGE that neither when it was over nor a long time afterward did he regret that night. Looking at it from the perspective of ten years, the fact that Judy's flare for him endured just one month seemed of little importance. Nor did it matter that by his yielding he subjected himself to a deeper agony in the end and gave serious hurt to Irene Scheerer and to Irene's parents, who had befriended him. There was nothing sufficiently pictorial about Irene's grief to stamp itself on his mind.

Dexter was at bottom hard-minded. The attitude of the city on his action was of no importance to him, not because he was going to leave the city, but because any outside attitude on the situation seemed superficial. He was completely indifferent to popular opinion. Nor, when he had seen that it was no use, that he did not possess in himself the power to move fundamentally or to hold Judy Jones,

26

did he bear any malice toward her. He loved her, and he would love her until the day he was too old for loving—but he could not have her. So he tasted the deep pain that is reserved only for the strong, just as he had tasted for a little while the deep happiness.

Even the ultimate falsity of the grounds upon which Judy terminated the engagement that she did not want to "take him away" from Irene — Judy, who had wanted nothing else — did not revolt him. He was beyond any revulsion or any amusement.

He went East in February with the intention of selling out his laundries and settling in New York—but the war came to America in March and changed his plans. He returned to the West, handed over the management of the business to his partner, and went into the first officers' training-camp in late April. He was one of those young thousands who greeted the war with a certain amount of relief, welcoming the liberation from webs of tangled emotion.

VI

THIS STORY is not his biography, remember, although things creep into it which have nothing to do with those dreams he had when he was young. We are almost done with them and with him now. There is only one more incident to be related here, and it happens seven years farther on.

It took place in New York, where he had done well—so well that there were no barriers too high for him. He was thirty-two years old, and, except for one flying trip immediately after the war, he had not been West in seven years. A man named Devlin from Detroit came into his office to see him in a business way, and then and there this incident occurred, and closed out, so to speak, this particular side of his life.

"So you're from the Middle West," said the man Devlin with careless curiosity. "That's funny — I thought men like you were probably born and raised on Wall Street. You know — wife of one of my best friends in Detroit came from your city. I was an usher at the wedding."

Dexter waited with no apprehension of what was coming.

"Judy Simms," said Devlin with no particular interest; "Judy Jones she was once."

"Yes, I knew her." A dull impatience spread over him. He had heard, of course, that she was married — perhaps deliberately he had heard no more.

"Awfully nice girl," brooded Devlin meaninglessly, "I'm sort of sorry for her."

"Why?" Something in Dexter was alert, receptive, at once.

"Oh, Lud Simms has gone to pieces in a way. I don't mean he ill-uses her, but he drinks and runs around "

"Doesn't she run around?"

"No. Stays at home with her kids."

"Oh."

27

"She's a little too old for him," said Devlin.

"Too old!" cried Dexter. "Why, man, she's only twenty-seven."

He was possessed with a wild notion of rushing out into the streets and taking a train to Detroit. He rose to his feet spasmodically.

"I guess you're busy," Devlin apologized quickly. "I didn't realize ——"

"No, I'm not busy," said Dexter, steadying his voice. "I'm not busy at all. Not busy at all. Did you say she was—twenty-seven? No, I said she was twenty-seven."

"Yes, you did," agreed Devlin dryly.

"Go on, then. Go on."

"What do you mean?"

"About Judy Jones."

Devlin looked at him helplessly.

"Well, that's, I told you all there is to it. He treats her like the devil. Oh, they're not going to get divorced or anything. When he's particularly outrageous she forgives him. In fact, I'm inclined to think she loves him. She was a pretty girl when she first came to Detroit."

A pretty girl! The phrase struck Dexter as ludicrous.

"Isn't she — a pretty girl, any more?"

"Oh, she's all right."

"Look here," said Dexter, sitting down suddenly, "I don't understand. You say she was a 'pretty girl' and now you say she's 'all right.' I don't understand what you mean—Judy Jones wasn't a pretty girl, at all. She was a great beauty. Why, I knew her, I knew her. She was ——"

Devlin laughed pleasantly.

"I'm not trying to start a row," he said. "I think Judy's a nice girl and I like her. I can't understand how a man like Lud Simms could fall madly in love with her, but he did." Then he added: "Most of the women like her."

Dexter looked closely at Devlin, thinking wildly that there must be a reason for this, some insensitivity in the man or some private malice.

"Lots of women fade just like that," Devlin snapped his fingers. "You must have seen it happen. Perhaps I've forgotten how pretty she was at her wedding. I've seen her so much since then, you see. She has nice eyes."

A sort of dulness settled down upon Dexter. For the first time in his life he felt like getting very drunk. He knew that he was laughing loudly at something Devlin had said, but he did not know what it was or why it was funny. When, in a few minutes, Devlin went he lay down on his lounge and looked out the window at the New York sky-line into which the sun was sinking in dull lovely shades of pink and gold.

He had thought that having nothing else to lose he was invulnerable at last—but he knew that he had just lost something more, as surely as if he had married Judy Jones and seen her fade away before his eyes.

The dream was gone. Something had been taken from him. In a sort of panic he pushed the palms of his hands into his eyes and tried to bring up a picture of the waters lapping on Sherry Island and the moonlit veranda, and gingham on the golf-links and the dry sun and the gold color of her neck's soft down. And her mouth damp to his kisses and her eyes plaintive with melancholy and her freshness like new fine linen in the morning. Why, these things were no longer in the world! They had existed and they existed no longer.

For the first time in years the tears were streaming down his face. But they were for himself now. He did not care about mouth and eyes and moving hands. He wanted to care, and he could not care. For he had gone away and he could never go back any more. The gates were closed, the sun was gone down, and there was no beauty but the gray beauty of steel that withstands all time. Even the grief he could have borne was left behind in the country of illusion, of youth, of the richness of life, where his winter dreams had flourished.

"Long ago," he said, "long ago, there was something in me, but now that thing is gone. Now that thing is gone, that thing is gone. I cannot cry. I cannot care. That thing will come back no more."

Answer *true* **or** *false* **for each of the following statements.**

1.65 _____ Dexter first meets Judy when he is fourteen and a caddie at the golf course.

1.66 _____ Dexter's winter dreams were concerned with the attainment of "glittering things."

1.67 _____ After college, Dexter bought a partnership in a gas station and lost all of his money.

1.68 _____ Dexter sees Judy again while playing golf with the men for whom he used to caddie as a boy.

1.69 _____ Judy introduces herself to Dexter while he is relaxing on a raft on the lake and soon after invites him to dinner at her house.

1.70 _____ After she kisses him, Dexter realizes that he does not want to be around her.

1.71 _____ Dexter is forced to see Judy in a "different light" when she disappears in a roadster with another man.

1.72 _____ Judy did not have "many youthful lovers."

1.73 _____ Just before his twenty-fourth summer, Dexter realizes that Judy will marry him.

1.74 _____ Dexter remains obsessed with Judy even after he is engaged to Irene Scheerer.

1.75 _____ Judy can't understand why she can't be happy.

1.76 _____ Dexter regrets breaking his engagement with Irene for a one-month relationship with Judy.

1.77 _____ Devlin can't understand why a man like Lud Simms could fall madly in love with Judy.

1.78 _____ Dexter's image of Judy is shattered because she is no longer a "glittering" beauty.

1.79 _____ Dexter's winter dreams had flourished in the "country of illusion."

1.80 _____ At the end of the story, Dexter is more alive than in his youth; he is able to care and to feel as never before.

Review the material in this section in preparation for the Self-Test, which will check your mastery of this particular section. The items missed on this Self-Test will indicate specific areas where restudy is necessary for mastery.

SELF-TEST 1

Answer *true* **or** *false* **for each of the following statements** (each answer, 2 points).

1.01 _____ World War I proved that society had succeeded in bringing peace and happiness to everyone.

1.02 _____ The large-scale loss of life in World War I caused writers to be optimistic.

1.03 _____ After the war, Americans were content with traditional manners and beliefs.

1.04 _____ The 1930s were known as the Jazz Age.

1.05 _____ Popular culture helped to spread the desire for social permissiveness and the pursuit of pleasure.

1.06 _____ The automobile had little effect on American society and culture.

1.07 _____ The Eighteenth Amendment to the U.S. Constitution was largely obeyed.

1.08 _____ Political oppression brought occupational and educational independence for women.

1.09 _____ Sigmund Freud theorized that all of man's problems stem from satisfied desires.

1.010 _____ In October 1929, the stock market crash left millions of people jobless and hungry.

1.011 _____ During the 1930s, communism was popular among union workers and the intellectual elite.

1.012 _____ In the midst of the Depression, the New Deal provided welfare funds for the unemployed, promised social security for the old and disabled, and created millions of jobs in the public sector.

1.013 _____ The depression of the 1930s was felt worldwide, creating social unrest in Europe and the opportunity for the rise of fascist leaders.

1.014 _____ At the heart of the Fundamentalist/Modernist controversy was the Bible.

1.015 _____ Religious Modernists argued for a faith more compliant to the advances in modern science and the changing culture.

1.016 _____ After World War I, art began to reflect the pessimism and discontinuity of the modern age.

1.017 _____ Modernism assumed that the world had moved into a post-Christian era.

1.018 _____ Almost every writer of significance traveled to London in search of the artistic support that was lacking at home.

Fill in each of the blanks using items from the following word list (each answer, 2 points).

| depression | Zelda's | emptiness | conservative | socializing | clear | nouns |
| screenwriting | Hollywood | Paris | hunting | mental | adjectives |

1.019 Ernest Hemingway was born and raised in a stronghold of _____ politics and morality.

1.020 Hemingway moved with his wife to _____ to further his career as a writer.

1.021 An adaptation of his journalistic experience, Hemingway's writing style is _____ and precise.

AMERICAN LITERATURE

LIFEPAC TEST

89 / 111

Name _____

Date _____

Score _____

AMERICAN LITERATURE LIFEPAC FOUR TEST

Underline the correct answer in each of the following statements (each answer, 3 points).

1. Ernest Hemingway's writing style is (clear and precise, muddled and rambling, slurred and meaningless).

2. Hemingway avoided (nouns, adjectives, sentences) and focused on the weight of his nouns.

3. F. Scott Fitzgerald's characters are troubled by an (pot hole, emptiness, financial debt) they cannot fill.

4. Unable to find an answer to the world's problems in politics, W. H. Auden turned to (gambling, religion, drugs).

5. "The Unknown Citizen" is a (comedy, satire, tragedy) of modern problems.

6. The poetry of (E. E. Cummings, W. H. Auden, Langston Hughes) captures the rhythms of jazz and blues.

7. Hughes inspired other (white, Italian, black) writers to take pride in their cultural roots.

8. Hughes' work helped to provide a lasting place for black writers in (French, Italian, American) literature.

9. Curtains and scenery are not used in (T. S. Eliot's, E. E. Cummings', Wilder's) plays.

Answer *true* or *false* for each of the following statements (each answer, 2 points).

10. _____ The Bible had nothing to do with the Fundamentalist/Modernist controversy.

11. _____ World War I proved that society and its traditional beliefs and manners were still useful.

12. _____ After World War I, art began to reflect the optimism and continuity of Ancient Rome.

13. _____ Modernism assumed that the world had moved into a new Christian era.

14. _____ In Ernest Hemingway's short story "In Another Country," the hospital patients are hooked up to machines to heal their wounds.

15. _____ In F. Scott Fitzgerald's short story "Winter Dreams," Dexter Green's winter dreams were concerned with the attainment of a family.

16. _____ Faces are compared to petals on the sidewalk in the poem "In a Station of the Metro."

17. _____ In his poem "Chicago," Carl Sandburg uses traditional verse.

18. _____ In the poem "Anecdote of the Jar," the hill symbolizes the imagination.

19. _____ In Frost's poem, "Mending Wall," the speaker repeats the cliche, "Good fences make good neighbors."

20. _____ In "The Unknown Citizen," W. H. Auden is criticizing modern society because it is impersonal.

21. _____ In "The Trumpet Player," the music is described as "bitterness/ Mixed with soap."

22. _____ The rhythm is described as "agony/ Distilled from old desire."

23. _____ In the play "Our Town," the stage directions don't call for a curtain.

24. _____ Mrs. Gibbs tells the audience that in the future Joe Crowell Jr. dies in France during the war.

25. _____ Mr. Webb describes Grover's Corners as an extraordinary town.

26. _____ The Stage Manager wants to get a copy of the play placed in the cornerstone of the new bank so that people a thousand years from now will know a few simple facts about Grover's Corners.

27. _____ The Christian gospel is an account of how God saves man.

28. _____ Liberalism and Christianity have different concepts of God and man.

29. _____ Christianity begins with an optimistic view of man.

30. _____ Salvation, according to the Bible, depends solely upon your feelings and experience in the present.

31. _____ Christianity is founded upon the shifting emotions of sinful men, otherwise known as "experience."

32. _____ At the center of Christianity is the doctrine of "justification by faith."

33. _____ Christianity says that our obedience to God's law is the ground of hope.

Fill in each of the blanks using items from the following word list (each answer, 2 points).

man	delight	working
farm life	wisdom	jazz and blues
fundamentalism's	images	traditional
imagism	inerrancy	free
interpretation	modernists	compresses
familiar	modernist	poetry

34. The modernist style _____ emotion and narration.

35. The modernist movement saw truth as a matter of _____ .

36. Black writers of the Harlem Renaissance carried the rhythms of _____ music over into various forms of literature.

37. Ezra Pound's experimental techniques and forms had no regard for

_____ ideas and approaches.

38. Pound was a central figure in the _____ movement.

39. Pound's most influential form of poetry was called _____ .

40. Imagism focused on concrete _____ rather than abstractions.

41. Carl Sandburg wrote about the struggles and triumphs of the _____ class.

42. Sandburg's use of _____ verse form made his poems easy to grasp.

43. E. E. Cummings used traditional forms to view the _____ in a new way.

44. Wallace Stevens believed that _____ was the highest human activity.

45. According to Stevens, the imagination of _____ is that which shapes reality.

46. As a traditional poet, Frost believed that poetry should begin in _____

and end with _____ .

47. Frost's poems are replete with images of _____ .

48. As an advocate of the _____ of Scripture, J. Gresham Machen was

_____ "most prominent champion" in the 1930s.

49.   *Christianity and Liberalism,* Machen's most well-known book, argued that
_____ were not preaching the gospel but had created a new religion.

Thinking and Writing

Choose one of the following "Thought and Discussion" topics.
Write your answer on a separate piece of paper.

1. Explain the controversy between the fundamentalists and the modernists (liberal Protestants).
    Be sure to give a brief summary of J. Gresham Machen's comparison of Christianity and liberalism. Your summary should include the different views of God, man, and the way of salvation.
    Discuss the importance of the Bible in determining both what the Christian faith is and what it is not.

2. Explain the despair and helplessness that many modern writers and artists felt.
    Recall the fact that Ernest Hemingway and Ezra Pound experienced mental problems.
    In light of Galatians 5:19–26, discuss how sin causes despair?
    From where does hope and happiness come?
    Explain how modern society has fostered feelings of despair and helplessness in people.

3. Reflecting upon Proverbs 5 and 7, explain Dexter Green's life and his relationship with Judy Jones in Fitzgerald's short story "Winter Dreams." Discuss the similarities between the woman in Proverbs 5 and 7 and Judy Jones. Be sure to include in your discussion how Dexter went down to the "chambers of death" and the ways in which he could have lived a happier life.

1.022   Hemingway avoided _____ and focused on the weight of his _____ .

1.023   As an international celebrity, Hemingway traveled the world _____ wild game and _____ in famous bars.

1.024   Hemingway frequently suffered from bouts of _____ .

1.025   Fitzgerald's characters are troubled by an _____ that they cannot fill.

1.026   Fitzgerald wrote *This Side of Paradise* to win _____ hand in marriage.

1.027   In 1930 Zelda was placed in a _____ institution, where she stayed until the end of her life.

1.028   In 1937 Fitzgerald moved to _____ to pursue a career in _____ .

Answer *true* or *false* for each of the following statements (each answer, 3 points).

1.029   _____   In the short story "In Another Country," hospital patients are hooked up to machines to heal their wounds.

1.030   _____   The major waited to marry his wife until he was out of the war.

1.031   _____   Hopeful of full recovery, the major stares at the photographs of the cured hands.

1.032   _____   In "Winter Dreams," Dexter's winter dreams were concerned with the attainment of "glittering things."

1.033   _____   Dexter is forced to see Judy in a "different light" when she disappears in a roadster with another man.

1.034   _____   Dexter remains obsessed with Judy even after he is engaged to Irene Scheerer.

1.035   _____   Dexter's image of Judy is shattered because she is no longer a "glittering" beauty.

1.036   _____   Dexter's winter dreams had flourished in the "country of illusion."

Underline the correct answer in each of the following statements (each answer, 3 points).

1.037   An economy of words is reflective of the (traditional, biblical, modernist) style of prose.

1.038   The modernist style (expands, compresses, exaggerates) emotion and narration.

1.039   In the modernist movement, truth was a matter of (biblical standard, historical record, interpretation).

1.040   Black writers of the Harlem Renaissance carried the rhythm of (jazz and blues, baroque, classical) music over into various forms of literature.

1.041   The Harlem Renaissance was an attempt by (black, Hispanic, Italian) writers to establish a cultural center equal to that of the whites in Paris.

For Thought and Discussion

Read Proverbs 5 and 7 with a parent or a teacher. Explain Dexter Green's life and his relationship with Judy Jones in Fitzgerald's short story "Winter Dreams." Discuss the similarities between the woman in Proverbs 5 and 7 and Judy Jones. Be sure to talk about how Dexter went down to the "chambers of death" and the ways in which he could have lived a happier life.

81 / 101

Score   _____

Teacher check   _____
                                  Initial   Date

II. MODERN POETRY

Ezra Pound (1885–1972). An often controversial figure, Ezra Pound urged the writers of his time to "make it new." His experimental techniques and forms had no regard for traditional ideas and approaches. Yet, he possessed a deep attachment to the poets of the past. Contradiction was a part of both his life and his work, which he said could not be separated. Although charged with treason and diagnosed as insane, he made significant contributions to American literature. Most modern American poetry and prose shows his influence.

Pound was born in Hailey, Idaho, but was raised in a suburb of Philadelphia. He attended the University of Pennsylvania and Hamilton College. He hoped to support himself as a teacher while he continued to write, but after only six months of teaching, he was dismissed on charges of indiscretionary behavior. Disgusted with his treatment as an artist, Pound moved to Europe. He believed that America had no culture and no place for art. He lived in London and Paris and became a central figure in the modernist movement. His ideas and work influenced British and American writers such as William Butler Yeats, Ernest Hemingway, T. S. Eliot, Robert Frost, and H.D.—the pen name used by Hilda Doolittle.

His most influential form of poetry was called "imagism." He persuaded a handful of writers to follow its rules and produce works that focused on concrete images rather than abstractions. The Imagists wrote with an economy of words, evoking a single emotion. They chose their words with precision. They created new rhythms with the use of everyday language. Unlike traditional poets, the imagists often created for the sake of art. In other words, their work often had no stated purpose or meaning. Imagist poetry was not written to teach the reader about the world but to move the emotions. A collection of the imagists' works was first published in 1914 with the French title *Des Imagistes.* The movement, however, was short-lived. Soon after, in 1915, Pound began working on *The Cantos.* Eventually 116 separate poems, it is a collection of Pound's views on history, politics, and literature.

In 1925 Pound settled in a small town in Italy. Convinced that art would "flourish" only in an environment ruled by a strong leader, he supported the fascist dictator Benito Mussolini during World War II. In several radio addresses on behalf of the Italian government, he attacked President Franklin D. Roosevelt and American society. In 1943 he was charged with treason and taken into captivity by U.S. troops. Before being taken to trial, he was judged "insane and mentally unfit." Pound was then confined to St. Elizabeth's Hospital for the criminally insane. With the help of devoted friends and congressmen, he was released in 1958 and allowed to return to Italy. Until his death, he continued to criticize America and urge its people to "make it new."

 Underline the correct answer in each of the following statements.

2.1   Ezra Pound's experimental techniques and forms had no regard for (modern, traditional, progressive) ideas and approaches.

2.2   Pound was a central figure in the (traditionalist, fundamentalist, modernist) movement.

2.3   His most influential form of poetry was called (imagism, traditionalism, communism).

2.4   Imagism focused on concrete (impressions, images, types) rather than abstractions.

2.5   The Imagists used (many, few) words to evoke a single emotion.

2.6   Imagism used (formal, traditional, everyday) language.

2.7   The works of the Imagists often did not have any (rhythm, meaning, words).

2.8   Pound's (*The Cantos, The Waste Land, In a Station of the Metro*) is a collection of views on history, politics, and literature.

2.9   During World War II, Pound made several radio addresses in support of the (American, British, Italian) government.

2.10   Pound was charged with (treason, murder, theft).

2.11   Before being taken to trial, Pound was judged (sane, insane, happy).

What to Look For:

Imagism sought to evoke a single emotion or response by using an economy of words. Pound's poem "In a Station in the Metro" is a famous example of imagism. (The Metro is the subway system in Paris.) As you read, notice the effects of the imagist poem on your mind and emotions. What images rush into your head? How do those images make you feel? Does the poem teach you anything? Is there a "moral to the story?"

In a Station of the Metro

The apparition of these faces in the crowd;
Petals on a wet, black bough.

by Ezra Pound, –reprinted with permission Copyright © New Directions Publishing Corp.

Answer *true* or *false* for each of the following statements.

2.12   _____ The poem is about the images you would see in a park in New York City.

2.13   _____ The faces are compared to petals.

2.14   _____ The tree branch is white.

2.15   _____ The faces look like petals stuck together on a tree branch.

2.16   _____ The moral of the story is to stay away from trees.

Carl Sandburg (1878–1967). Once called the "laureate of industrial America," Carl Sandburg wrote about the struggles and triumphs of the working class. His free verse form made his poems easy to grasp and popular with the general public. (Free verse is an unconventional form of poetry that does not use meter and rhyme.) Sandburg described his work as "simple poems for simple people."

Born to Swedish immigrants in Galesburg, Illinois, Sandburg declared at an early age, "I'm going to be a writer." But poor beginnings and a desire to travel the open road delayed his rise to popularity. He attended school irregularly, never completing his college degree. After working odd jobs around the country, he moved to Chicago in 1913. He worked as a journalist while attempting to create poetry that captured the energy of the people. In 1914, *Poetry* magazine published his poem "Chicago." He followed the poem's success by publishing four volumes of poems in eight years: *Chicago Poems* (1916), *Cornhuskers* (1918), *Smoke and Steel* (1920), and *Slabs of the Sunburnt West* (1922).

Sandburg's interest in the spirit of the American working class also led him to write a multivolume biography of Abraham Lincoln for which he won the Pulitzer Prize in 1940. Sandburg earned a second Pulitzer Prize in 1951 for his *Complete Poems*.

He also toured the country as a folk singer, endearing himself to the American people. In 1927 he published a collection of American folk songs, *The American Songbag*. Always close to the common people, President Lyndon Johnson eulogized him thus: "Carl Sandburg was more than the voice of America, more than the poet of its strength and genius. He was America."

Underline the correct answer in each of the following statements.

2.17   Carl Sandburg wrote about the struggles and triumphs of the (upper, working, middle) class.

2.18   His use of (free, traditional, experimental) verse form made his poems easy to grasp.

2.19   Before moving to (Chicago, Detroit, New York City) in 1913, Sandburg worked odd jobs around the country.

2.20   From 1916 to 1922, Sandburg published (two, four, six) volumes of poems.

2.21   Sandburg won a Pulitzer Prize for his multivolume biography of (Thomas Jefferson, Jane Adams, Abraham Lincoln).

2.22   In 1951 Sandburg won a Pulitzer Prize for his (*Chicago Poems*, *Complete Poems*, *Cornhuskers*).

2.23   Sandburg toured the country as a (congressman, shoe salesman, folk singer).

What to Look For:

Sandburg wrote in free verse. He used everyday language powerfully and vividly. As you read the following poem, examine Sandburg's realistic description of Chicago. Does he convey a sense of shame or pride? Considering the city's wicked characteristics, what *should* Sandburg's reaction be? How does Sandburg's modern view of man conflict with Proverbs 6:16–19?

Chicago

HOG Butcher for the World,
Tool Maker, Stacker of Wheat,
Player with Railroads and the Nation's Freight Handler;
Stormy, husky, brawling,
City of the Big Shoulders:

They tell me you are wicked and I believe them, for I
    have seen your painted women under the gas lamps
    luring the farm boys.
And they tell me you are crooked and I answer: Yes, it
    is true I have seen the gunman kill and go free to
    kill again.
And they tell me you are brutal and my reply is: On the
    faces of women and children I have seen the marks
    of wanton hunger.
And having answered so I turn once more to those who
    sneer at this my city, and I give them back the sneer
    and say to them:
Come and show me another city with lifted head singing
    so proud to be alive and coarse and strong and cunning.
Flinging magnetic curses amid the toil of piling job on
    job, here is a tall bold slugger set vivid against the
    little soft cities;

Fierce as a dog with tongue lapping for action, cunning
    as a savage pitted against the wilderness,
        Bareheaded,
        Shoveling,
        Wrecking,
        Planning,
        Building, breaking, rebuilding,
Under the smoke, dust all over his mouth, laughing with
    white teeth,
Under the terrible burden of destiny laughing as a young
    man laughs,
Laughing even as an ignorant fighter laughs who has
    never lost a battle,
Bragging and laughing that under his wrist is the pulse.
    and under his ribs the heart of the people, Laughing!
Laughing the stormy, husky, brawling laughter of
    Youth, half-naked, sweating, proud to be Hog
    Butcher, Tool Maker, Stacker of Wheat, Player with
    Railroads and Freight Handler to the Nation.

Answer *true* **or** *false* **for each of the following statements.**

2.24 _____ "Chicago" is written in traditional verse.

2.25 _____ The speaker calls Chicago the "City of the Big Shoulders" and
the "Chicken Butcher for the World."

2.26 _____ In lines 6, 7, and 8, "they" tell the speaker that Chicago is "wicked,"
"crooked," and "brutal."

2.27 _____ The speaker smiles back at those who "sneer" at his city.

2.28 _____ In the second stanza, the speaker uses long lines of free verse
or everyday language.

2.29 _____ In the third stanza, the speaker applies human qualities to the city
by describing the different ways it "laughs."

2.30 _____ The descriptive list in lines 1–4 is found again in the last four lines.

E. E. Cummings (1894–1962). As an individualist,
E. E. Cummings used experimental forms to affirm the
unique and criticize the artificial. His unconventional
use of punctuation, capitalization, and formatting affect
the reader visually. The appearance of his poetry
speaks of his modernism more so than his actual
themes. He wrote about traditional subjects, preferring to write in a simple manner. His humor and his
attention to relationships made his work popular.

Born in Cambridge, Massachusetts, and a graduate
of Harvard, Edward Estlin Cummings was the prod-
uct of high-breed culture and institutionalized unbe-
lief. Educated in the classics, Cummings developed
his unconventional techniques out of a connection
with the past. He sought to express the traditional
in a visually exciting manner.

At the outbreak of World War I, Cummings joined the ambulance corps. But after a misunderstanding with French authorities, he found himself imprisoned for three months under suspicion of treason. Out of his experiences in the detention camp and his frustration with bureaucracy, Cummings wrote his book *The Enormous Room* (1922).

After the war, Cummings sought to develop himself as a writer and an artist. He lived in Paris and became acquainted with Pablo Picasso. He also meet Ezra Pound, who heavily influenced his poetry. Upon returning to the United States, Cummings lived in an apartment in Greenwich Village (an artists' colony in the heart of New York City) and spent summers on his family's farm in New Hampshire.

Critics did not readily receive Cummings' work. Some of them rejected his techniques as "visual tricks." But eventually he was appreciated as a poet who understood the culture's increasing reliance upon visual stimulation. Cummings dealt with modern society's fragmentation and confusion with humor and irony. Although he wrote about traditional themes and detested the conveniences of modern life, his lifestyle was progressively immoral. Championing the freedom of the individual, he celebrated sensuality and unashamedly wrote of his lack of moral integrity.

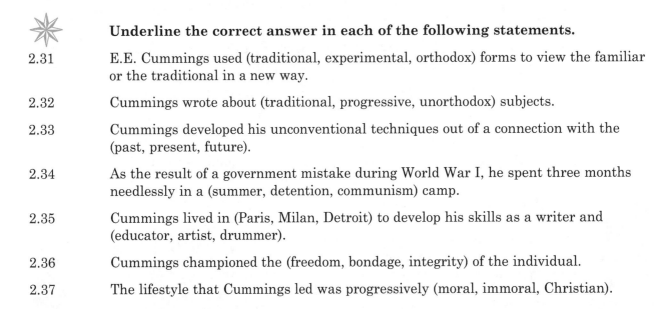

During his lifetime, he completed four volumes of poetry. He was awarded the Bollingen Prize in 1957.

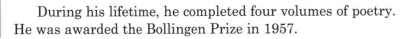

Underline the correct answer in each of the following statements.

2.31   E.E. Cummings used (traditional, experimental, orthodox) forms to view the familiar or the traditional in a new way.

2.32   Cummings wrote about (traditional, progressive, unorthodox) subjects.

2.33   Cummings developed his unconventional techniques out of a connection with the (past, present, future).

2.34   As the result of a government mistake during World War I, he spent three months needlessly in a (summer, detention, communism) camp.

2.35   Cummings lived in (Paris, Milan, Detroit) to develop his skills as a writer and (educator, artist, drummer).

2.36   Cummings championed the (freedom, bondage, integrity) of the individual.

2.37   The lifestyle that Cummings led was progressively (moral, immoral, Christian).

What to Look For:

Cummings sought to express the traditional in a visually exciting manner. He was an experimentalist. As you read the following selections, examine his unusual use of punctuation and visual arrangement. Are these techniques merely "visual tricks?"

ḭn Just—

spring   when the world is mud-
luscious the little
lame balloonman

whistles   far   and wee   5

and eddieanbill come
running from marbles and
piracies and it's
spring

when the world is puddle-wonderful   10

the queer
old balloonman whistles
far   and   wee
and bettyandisbel come dancing

from hop-scotch and jump-rope and   15

it's
spring
and
    the

            goat-footed   20
balloonMan   whistles
far
and
wee

by: E. E. Cummings, –reprinted with permission Copyright © Liveright Publishing Co.

---

r-p-o-p-h-e-s-s-a-g-r
The word grasshopper is scrambled in lines 1, 5, and 12. To understand the poem, read grasshopper
correctly and ignore the punctuation marks. (Line 4 continues on line 6.)

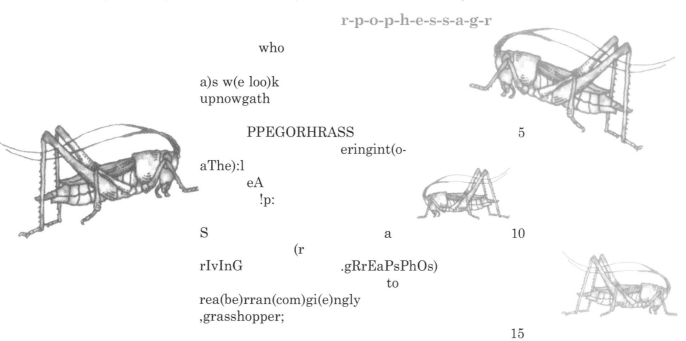

r-p-o-p-h-e-s-s-a-g-r

        who

a)s w(e loo)k
upnowgath

        PPEGORHRASS   5
                eringint(o-
aThe):l
    eA
        !p:

S   a   10
        (r
rIvInG   .gRrEaPsPhOs)
                    to
rea(be)rran(com)gi(e)ngly
,grasshopper;

                                            15

by: E. E. Cummings, –reprinted with permission Copyright © Liveright Publishing Co.

Written normally, this poem reads, "Grasshopper who as we look up now gathering into a—The leap!,
arriving to rearrangingly become grasshopper."

37

Answer *true* or *false* for each of the following statements.

2.38 _____ The season that is spoken of in the poem "in Just–" is winter.

2.39 _____ Each time the "balloonman" is mentioned, different adjectives are used to describe him.

2.40 _____ When the "balloonman" whistles, "eddieandbill" and "bettyandisbel" are aroused to action.

2.41 _____ In "r-p-o-p-h-e-s-s-a-g-r" the word *bug* is scrambled in lines 1, 5, and 14.

2.42 _____ The visual arrangement of "r-p-o-p-h-e-s-s-a-g-r" centers around its subject: "The leap!"

Wallace Stevens (1879–1955). Wallace Stevens believed that poetry was the highest human activity. Awash in the chaos of the modern era, he looked to art to make sense out of the world. For Stevens and many other writers of his time, art had replaced religion.

Stevens, though he left Harvard early to pursue a literary career, was determined not to "make a petty struggle for existence." For many years, no one knew he wrote poetry. Like his father, he worked a regular full-time job during the day and wrote poetry at night. After failing to make it as a journalist, he returned to school. He completed a degree in law and worked for Hartford Accident and Indemnity Company in Hartford, Connecticut, until his death.

Not until 1923, at the age of forty-four, did Stevens publish his first volume of poems, *Harmonium.* His work is a dazzling display of wit and imagery. As one critic observed, in his brief lyrics, Stevens demonstrates the power of the imagination in its ability to observe the beauty of nature while expressing his belief that same beauty is dependent upon the perception of the observer. Stevens did not hold that there was such a thing as absolute beauty or absolute truth. He believed that man and his imagination are what shape reality, not God. Laboring under this conviction, he believed that his poetry could "help people live their lives" and understand the modern world.

Stevens went on to publish several more volumes of poetry. His *Collected Poems* (1955) earned him the Pulitzer Prize.

Underline the correct answer in each of the following statements.

2.43 Wallace Stevens believed that (poetry, worship, singing) was the highest human activity.

2.44 Stevens worked a (consulting, part-time, regular full-time) job during the day and wrote poetry at night.

2.45 In 1923 at the age of forty-four, Stevens published his (first, second, third,) volume of poems.

2.46 Stevens's poems demonstrate the power of the (imagination, truth, Word of God).

2.47 Stevens believed that beauty was (independent of, dependent upon) the perception of the observer.

2.48 (God, Man) and his imagination is what shapes reality, according to Stevens.

2.49 Because (art, religion) had replaced (art, religion), Stevens (doubted, believed) that his poetry could "help people live their lives."

2.50 Stevens earned the (Nobel, Pulitzer, Bollingen) Prize for his *Collected Poems.*

What to Look For:

Wallace Stevens believed that the imagination was the key to understanding reality. What does the jar-represent? Can it represent more than one thing? What does the jar's multiple meanings convey about reality? Do Stevens, and the other modernists, believe that reality has no concrete meaning?

Anecdote of the Jar

I placed a jar in Tennessee,
And round it was, upon a hill.
It made the slovenly wilderness
Surround that hill.
The wilderness rose up to it,
And sprawled around, no longer wild.
The jar was round upon the ground
And tall and of a port in air.
It took dominion every where.
The jar was gray and bare.
It did not give of bird or bush,
Like nothing else in Tennessee.

by Wallace Stevens, –reprinted with permission Copyright © Alfred A. Knopf, Inc.

One interpretation of the poem says that the jar represents the imagination. Another interpretation sees the jar as a symbol of civilization and its effects on nature. But both interpretations see human invention as the key to the appearance of nature; our mind is what shapes reality.

Answer *true* **or** *false* **for each of the following statements.**

2.51 _____ The jar can represent the imagination.

2.52 _____ The jar can symbolize civilization.

2.53 _____ The jar is placed in Missouri.

2.54 _____ God made the wilderness surround a hill.

2.55 _____ The wilderness rose up to the jar.

2.56 _____ God, the Creator, took dominion everywhere.

2.57 _____ The jar was "gray and bare."

2.58 _____ The jar gave the wilderness bird and bush.

2.59 _____ The jar was like nothing else in Tennessee.

2.60 _____ The jar shapes reality.

Robert Frost (1874–1963). By the end of his long life and enduring career as a poet, Robert Frost had received four Pulitzer Prizes. His use of traditional verse forms and the voice of a "wise country person," made him one of America's most beloved and well-known poets. But his success did not come until he was nearly forty.

Frost was born in California. His father died when he was eleven, causing the family to move to Lawrence, Massachusetts. His mother was a school teacher who loved literature. A poet herself, she encouraged Frost to write. After graduating from high school in 1891, Frost attended Dartmouth College and Harvard, but he never graduated. He found college life unappealing. Frost married Elinor White in 1894, and worked odd jobs. After the birth of four children, the family came into financial difficulties. Frost became abusive and then depressed. Wanting the means to pursue a career as a poet, he moved his family to England in 1912.

While living aboard, he developed a friendship with Ezra Pound, who reviewed his first collection of poems, *A Boy's Will* (1913), favorably. Frost published a second volume, *North of Boston,* in 1914. The works established Frost as an American poet. He returned to the United States in 1915 and was able to support his family with the sales of his books.

Frost's success and appeal as a poet brought him teaching jobs at Amherst, Dartmouth, Harvard, and the University of Michigan. He was awarded honorary degrees from nearly fifty universities. In 1960 John F. Kennedy asked him to read one of his poems at his presidential inauguration, the first time a poet was ever invited to do so.

As Frost rose in popularity, his desire to remain in rural New England never wavered. His poems are replete with images of farm life. Frost knew that his use of natural phenomena and traditional values would appeal to a shaken and disrupted generation. He said that poetry was a "momentary stay against confusion." But Frost's traditional verse and simple speaking voice can be deceiving. He was not the gentle New England farmer that is in his poetry. Rather, he created the persona for the purpose of persuasion. He believed that poetry should begin with delight and end with wisdom. Poetry was a method of teaching. Frost's practical advice spoken in the voice of a gentle farmer can seem appealing, but his wisdom is worldly. He did not acknowledge the sovereign rule of God. Frost's poems, therefore, should be read with much discernment.

 Underline the correct answer in each of the following statements.

2.61   Robert Frost received four (Pulitzer Prizes, Gold Medals, gold watches) during his lifetime.

2.62   He used (modern, traditional, free) verse forms and the voice of a (wise country, foolish city, humorous youth) person in his poetry.

2.63   He moved to New England when he was (one, eleven, forty).

2.64   To pursue a career as a poet, Frost moved his family to (France, Spain, England).

2.65   Frost's poems are replete with images of (city life, farm life, modern decay).

2.66   As a traditional poet, Frost believed that poetry should begin in (pain, agony, delight) and end with (ignorance, wisdom, confusion).

2.67   The wisdom of Frost's gentle farmer is (biblical, worldly, godly).

2.68   Frost thought that his (modern, traditional, free) verse would be appealing to moderns offering "momentary (movement, stay, instability) against the confusion."

What to Look For:

Robert Frost used traditional verse form, but he often questioned traditional beliefs. As you read the following poem, notice the subtle attack that he makes upon people who hold to traditional beliefs. How does the speaker criticize his neighbor's unwillingness to forsake his father's opinion about walls?

Mending Wall

Something there is that doesn't love a wall,
That sends the frozen-ground-swell under it,
And spills the upper boulders in the sun,
And makes gaps even two can pass abreast.
The work of hunters is another thing:
I have come after them and made repair
Where they have left not one stone on a stone,
But they would have the rabbit out of hiding,
To please the yelping dogs. The gaps I mean,
No one has seen them made or heard them made,
But at spring mending-time we find them there.
I let my neighbor know beyond the hill;
And on a day we meet to walk the line
And set the wall between us once again.
We keep the wall between us as we go.
To each the boulders that have fallen to each.
And some are loaves and some so nearly balls
We have to use a spell to make them balance:
'Stay where you are until our backs are turned!'
We wear our fingers rough with handling them.
Oh, just another kind of out-door game,
One on a side. It comes to little more:
There where it is we do not need the wall:
He is all pine and I am apple orchard.
My apple trees will never get across
And eat the cones under his pines, I tell him.
He only says, 'Good fences make good neighbors.'
Spring is the mischief in me, and I wonder
If I could put a notion in his head:
'Why do they make good neighbors? Isn't it
Where there are cows?
But here there are no cows.
Before I built a wall I'd ask to know
What I was walling in or walling out,
And to whom I was like to give offense.
Something there is that doesn't love a wall,
That wants it down.' I could say 'Elves' to him,
But it's not elves exactly, and I'd rather
He said it for himself. I see him there
Bringing a stone grasped firmly by the top
In each hand, like an old-stone savage armed.
He moves in darkness as it seems to me
Not of woods only and the shade of trees.

He will not go behind his father's saying,
And he likes having thought of it so well
He says again, "Good fences make good neighbors."

The wall in the poem represents more than a barrier between two neighboring farmers. It symbolizes traditional beliefs and opinions. The speaker can see no reason for the wall, but the speaker's neighbor insists that it is because his father (i.e., tradition) told him, "Good fences make good neighbors."

Answer *true* or *false* for each of the following statements.

2.69 _____ The gaps in the wall are caused by frozen-ground-swells and hunters.

2.70 _____ When it is time to mend the wall, the two neighbors walk on one side, repairing as they walk.

2.71 _____ The speaker does not see a need for a wall.

2.72 _____ The neighbor's only response to the speaker is, "Good fences make good neighbors."

2.73 _____ Before building a wall, the speaker would ask his father's opinion.

2.74 _____ According to lines 29 and 30, the speaker wishes that he could make his neighbor doubt his tradition of wall-mending.

2.75 _____ As the neighbor repairs the wall, the speaker describes him as a "old-stone savage armed."

2.76 _____ The neighbor insists that the wall is necessary because of his experiences.

2.77 _____ The wall symbolizes traditional beliefs and opinions.

W. H. Auden (1907–1973). Regarded by many as one of the most influential poets of the modern and postmodern eras, Wystan Hugh Auden saw value in traditional elements of life and poetry.

English by birth, Auden was educated at Oxford University, where he came into association with a group of politically active poets and intellectuals. His first book, *Poems* (1930), focused on the breakdown of English society. Expressing a concern for the individual in modern society, he wrote verse plays that included *The Dog Beneath the Sun* (1935) and *On the Frontier* (1938).

In 1939 Auden settled in the United States. The change marked a turning point in his life. Unable to find an answer for the world's problems in politics, he turned to religion. In his works *Double Man* (1941) and *For the Times Being* (1947) he implied that traditional beliefs, rather than communism, was the answer to modern fragmentation and disintegration. Auden's mother was a devout Anglo-Catholic, who probably influenced his change in perspective. In 1946 Auden became a naturalized citizen of the United States.

Auden's long narrative poem about life after World War II, *The Age of Anxiety* (1947), earned him the Pulitzer Prize in 1948. Auden went on to publish several volumes of poetry and to collaborate on a few opera librettos. As a modernist who was unwilling to relinquish all literary ties with the past, Auden resembles T. S. Eliot. His poem "The Unknown Citizen" is a satire of modern problems. It displays the influence of traditional forms of poetry on his work.

> **Fill in each of the blanks using items from the following word list.**

traditional	*The Age of Anxiety*	English
individual	Oxford	breakdown
religion	satire	

2.78   W.H. Auden saw value in _____ elements of life and poetry.

2.79   _____ by birth, Auden was educated at _____ University.

2.80   *Poems*, Auden's first book of poetry, focused on the _____ of English society.

2.81   Auden's verse plays reflect his concerns for the _____ in an increasingly conformist society.

2.82   Unable to find an answer for the world's problems in politics, Auden turned to _____ .

2.83   Auden earned the Pulitzer Prize in 1948 for his poem _____ .

2.84   "The Unknown Citizen" is a _____ of modern problems.

What to Look For:

"The Unknown Citizen" was written to criticize modern society by satirizing its increasingly impersonal environment. As you read, notice what type of details are known about the unknown citizen. Though much information is known about "the unknown citizen," why is he termed "unknown"?

The Unknown Citizen

by: W. H. Auden, –reprinted with permission Copyright © Random House, Inc.

He was found by the Bureau of Statistics to be
One against whom there was no official complaint,
And all the reports of his conduct agree
That, in the modern sense of the old-fashioned word, he was a saint,
For in everything he did he served the Greater Community.
Except for the war till the day he retired
He worked in a factory and never got fired,
But satisfied his employers, Fudge Motors Inc.
Yet he wasn't a scab or odd in his views,
For his union reports that he paid his dues,
(Our report of his union shows it was sound)
And our Social Psychology workers found
That he was popular with his mates and liked a drink.
The Press are convinced that he bought a paper every day,
And that his reactions to advertisements were normal in every way.
Policies taken out in his name prove that he was fully insured,
And his Health-card shows that he was once in hospital but left it cured.
Both Producers Research and High-Grade Living declare
He was fully sensible to the advantages of the Installment Plan
And had everything necessary to the Modern Man,
A gramophone, a radio, a car and a frigidaire.
Our researchers into Public Opinion are content
That he held the proper opinions for the time of the year;
When there was peace he was for peace; when there was war he went.
He was married and added five children to the population,
which our Eugenist says was the right number for a parent of his generation,
And our teachers report he never interfered with their education.
Was he free? Was he happy? The question is absurd:
Had anything been wrong, we should certainly have heard.

Answer *true* or *false* for each of the following statements.

2.85 _____ In "The Unknown Citizen" Auden is criticizing modern society because it is too personal.

2.86 _____ The only reason the unknown citizen was a "saint" was because there was no official complaint against him.

2.87 _____ His union reports said that he never paid his dues.

2.88 _____ The state's social psychology workers determined that he was well-liked and sociable.

2.89 _____ The press is sure that his reactions to advertisements were abnormal.

2.90 _____ Producers Research and High-Grade Living declared that he had everything necessary to the Modern Man.

2.91 _____ He always held opinions that were different than everyone else's.

2.92 _____ The eugenist said that he did not have enough children.

2.93 _____ Teachers reported that he never interfered with his children's education.

2.94 _____ The question of his freedom and happiness is absurd because the state would have known.

 Review the material in this section in preparation for the Self-Test, which will check both your mastery of this particular section and your knowledge of the previous section.

SELF-TEST 2

Underline the correct answer in each of the following statements (each answer, 2 points).

2.01 The modernist style (expands, compresses, exaggerates) emotion and narration.

2.02 The modernist movement saw truth as a matter of (biblical standard, historical record, interpretation).

2.03 Black writers of the Harlem Renaissance carried the rhythms of (jazz and blues, baroque, classical) music over into various forms of literature.

2.04 Ezra Pound's experimental techniques and forms had no regard for (modern, traditional, progressive) ideas and approaches.

2.05 Pound was a central figure in the (Traditionalist, Fundamentalist, Modernist) movement.

2.06 Pound's most influential form of poetry was called (imagism, traditionalism, communism).

2.07 Imagism focused on concrete (impressions, images, types) rather than abstractions.

2.08 The imagists used (many, few) words to evoke a single emotion.

2.09 Before being taken to trial for treason, Pound was judged to be (sane, insane, happy).

2.010 Carl Sandburg wrote about the struggles and triumphs of the (upper, working, middle) class.

2.011 Sandburg's use of (free, traditional, experimental) verse form made his poems easy to grasp.

2.012 E. E. Cummings used (traditional, experimental, orthodox) forms to view the familiar in a new way.

44

2.013   Cummings wrote about (traditional, progressive, unorthodox) subjects.

2.014   Cummings developed his unconventional techniques out of a connection with the (past, present, future).

2.015   Wallace Stevens believed that (poetry, worship, singing) was the highest human activity.

2.016   Stevens believed that beauty was (independent of, dependent upon) the perception of the observer.

2.017   According to Stevens, (God, Man) and his imagination is what shapes reality.

2.018   Frost used (modern, traditional, free) verse forms and the voice of a (wise country, foolish city, humorous young) person in his poetry.

2.019   Frost's poems are replete with images of (city life, farm life, modern decay).

2.020   As a traditional poet, Frost believed that poetry should begin in (pain, agony, delight) and end with (ignorance, wisdom, confusion).

Answer _true_ or _false_ for each of the following statements (each answer, 2 points).

2.021   _____   World War I proved that society and its traditional beliefs and manners had failed.

2.022   _____   After World War I, art began to reflect the pessimism and discontinuity of the modern age.

2.023   _____   Modernism assumed that the world had moved into a post-Christian era.

2.024   _____   In the poem "In a Station of the Metro," faces are compared to petals on a tree branch.

2.025   _____   In "Chicago," the speaker smiles at those who call the city "wicked," "crooked," and "brutal."

2.026   _____   In the second stanza of "Chicago," the speaker uses long lines of free verse or everyday language.

2.027   _____   The season that is spoken about in the poem "in Just–" is winter.

2.028   _____   When the "balloonman" whistles, "eddieandbill" and "bettyandisbel" are aroused to action.

2.029   _____   In "r-p-o-p-h-e-s-s-a-g-r," the word _bug_ is scrambled in lines 1, 5, and 14.

2.030   _____   In the poem "Anecdote of the Jar," the jar can symbolize the imagination.

2.031   _____   The jar shapes reality.

2.032   _____   In the poem "Mending Wall," the neighbor's only response to the speaker is, "Good fences make good neighbors."

2.033   _____   Before building a wall, the speaker would ask his father's opinion.

2.034   _____   The wall symbolizes traditional beliefs and opinions.

2.035   _____   In "The Unknown Citizen," Auden is criticizing modern society because it is too personal.

2.036   _____   The only reason the unknown citizen was thought to be a "saint" was because there was no official complaint against him.

2.037   _____   The question of the unknown citizen's freedom and happiness is absurd because the state would have known.

Fill in each of the blanks using items from the following word list (each answer, 4 points).

clear	traditional	satire
emptiness	religion	

2.038   Ernest Hemingway's writing style is _____ and precise.

2.039   F. Scott Fitzgerald's characters are troubled by an _____ they cannot fill.

2.040   W. H. Auden saw value in _____ elements of life and poetry.

2.041   Unable to find an answer for the world's problems in politics, Auden turned to

_____ .

2.042   "The Unknown Citizen" is a _____ of modern problems.

For Thought and Discussion.

Explain to a parent or a teacher the despair and helplessness that many modern writers and artists felt. Recall that Ernest Hemingway and Ezra Pound experienced mental problems. Read Galatians 5:19–26. Discuss how sin causes despair. From where does hope and happiness come? How has modern society fostered feelings of despair and helplessness in people?

Score _____

Teacher check _____

Initial   Date

III. OTHER MODERN AGE LITERATURE
HARLEM RENAISSANCE

Langston Hughes (1902–1967). As a leader of the Harlem Renaissance, Langston Hughes was its most popular poet. His work captured the rhythms of jazz and blues while portraying black life and its struggles in a largely prejudiced America. Hughes inspired other black writers to take pride in their cultural roots.

Hughes was born in Joplin, Missouri, and was raised by his maternal grandmother. During his high school years he lived with his mother in Cleveland. Hughes' mother encouraged him to write poetry, and he frequently contributed to the high school literary magazine. In 1921 he enrolled in Columbia University but only attended for a year. He traveled the world as a merchant seaman and worked menial jobs in Europe and the United States. However, Hughes continued to write poetry, and in 1925 he had several poems published in *The New Negro*, an anthology. His contributions won him the attention and the support of many whites, several people who were impressed helped finance his efforts until he was able to support himself by his writing.

His first book of poetry, *The Weary Blues*, was published in 1926. In 1932 he published another volume, *The Dream Keeper*. By this time the quality and passion of his work had earned him the title "the Shakespeare of Harlem." However, Hughes was also known as a spokesperson for the radical left. During the 1930s, he worked alongside Communist supporters and even published works in the *New Masses*, the Communist Party paper. Hughes' poem "Goodbye, Christ," reveals most poignantly, his misguided ideology. For a time, he believed that communism was the answer to racial injustice. Unfortunately, Hughes' attraction to communism and increasingly militancy led him to write many blasphemous poems.

Hughes' actual ideology is something of a mystery. But it is possible to conclude that he later regretted some of his more radical works. As one writer has noted, Hughes did not include most of these pieces in *Selected Poems*, published in 1951.

Hughes was not only a popular writer, he was also incredibly prolific. In addition to the sixteen volumes of poetry that Hughes published, he also wrote ten collections of short stories, nine children's books, over twenty-four works for the stage, two autobiographies, two novels, several film scripts, and a myriad of other works for popular consumption.

While working as a columnist for the Chicago *Defender*, a black weekly, Hughes created the simple minded yet wise persona, Jesse B. Semple. The character is one of his most noted contributions to American literature and culture. As one writer observed, Semple was similar in impact and influence as Mark Twain's Huck Finn. Semple first appeared in an op-ed piece by Hughes in 1943, and soon became a black folk hero. Hughes later included Semple in his 1963 musical play, *Simple Heaven*.

Convinced that art was the most effective weapon in the war against racial injustice, Hughes published the works of other black writers and established black theaters in both Chicago and Los Angeles. Though Hughes' radical ideology during the 1930s may have marred his reputation, nevertheless his use of black culture's rhythms and refrains in his poetry was nothing short of extraordinary. His work during the Harlem Renaissance provided hope for his people and a durable place for their roots in American literature.

Fill in each of the blanks using items from the following word list.

seaman	Columbia	world
mother	hero	cultural
Los Angeles	rhythm	American
film scripts	plays	

3.1   The poetry of Langston Hughes captures the _____ of jazz and blues.

3.2   Hughes's _____ encouraged him to write poetry.

3.3   He attended _____ University for a year.

3.4   He traveled the _____ for a year as a merchant _____.

3.5   In addition to his poems, Hughes published works of fiction, _____, autobiographies, and _____.

3.6   Jesse B. Semple became a black folk _____.

3.7   Hughes established black theatres in Chicago and _____.

3.8   Hughes inspired other black writers to take pride in their _____ roots.

3.9   His work helped to provide a lasting place for black writers in _____ literature.

What to Look For:

Langston Hughes captured the rhythms of jazz and blues in his poetry while portraying the struggles of black life in America. Read the following poem aloud. Listen for a beat in the repetition of words and phrases. Also, notice the way in which the speaker talks about his people. How does the speaker's passion match the beat?

Trumpet Player

The Negro
With the trumpet at his lips
Has dark moons of weariness
Beneath his eyes
Where the smoldering memory
Of slave ships
Blazed to the crack of whips
About his thighs.

The Negro
With the trumpet at his lips
Has a head of vibrant hair
Tamed down,
Patent-leathered now
Until it gleams
Like jet—
Were jet a crown.

The music
From the trumpet at his lips
Is honey
Mixed with liquid fire.
The rhythm
From the trumpet at his lips
Is ecstasy
Distilled with old desire—

Desire
That is longing for the moon
Where the moonlight's but a spotlight
In his eyes,
Desire
That is longing for the sea
Where the sea's a bar-glass
Sucker size.

The Negro
With the trumpet at his lips
Whose jacket
Has a fine one-button roll,
Does not know
Upon what riff the music slips
Its hypodermic needle
To his soul—

But softly
As the tune comes from his throat
Trouble
Mellows to a golden note.

by: Langston Hughes, –reprinted with permission Copyright © Knopf Publishing Group

Answer *true* **or** *false* **for each of the following statements.**

3.10 _____ The phrase "The Negro / with the trumpet at his lips" is repeated
in stanzas 1, 2, and 5.

3.11 _____ The trumpet player's "smoldering memory" is of parties on the beach.

3.12 _____ The music is described as "honey/ Mixed with liquid fire."

3.13 _____ The rhythm is described as "agony/ Distilled from new desire."

3.14 _____ In the fourth stanza, the word "Desire" is repeated.

3.15 _____ In the last stanza, trouble is "mellowed to a golden note."

DRAMA

Thornton Wilder (1897–1975). Thornton Wilder was a successful novelist and playwright. Using universal themes and straightforward language, his works were readily appreciated by the public. Wilder was born in Madison, Wisconsin, but because of his father's government job, he spent many of his childhood years in China. He earned his bachelor's degree from Yale and his master's degree from Princeton. He served as an officer in both World War I and World War II.

Wilder first reached success as a novelist, although his plays eventually brought him more recognition. In 1928 Wilder's second novel, *The Bridge at San Luis Rey,* earned him the Pulitzer Prize. Ten years later, Wilder proved his skills as a playwright, earning a second Pulitzer Prize for his play *Our Town.* He earned a third Pulitzer in 1943 for his play *The Skin of Our Teeth. The Matchmaker* was first performed in 1954, and later adapted in 1964 into the musical comedy *Hello Dolly!*

Many of Wilder's plays were considered experimental during his time. They call for no curtains and little scenery. A character in the

49

role of the Stage Manager gives the setting and continually comments to the audience on the action. By using this type of stage presentation, Wilder ensured that his audience would never forget that the play they were watching was not reality.

Despite the fact that it was unconventional, *Our Town* is one of Wilder's most reproduced plays. Theaters on Broadway and in small communities have produced it numerous times. Set in a rural New England town during the modern era, the play explores the meaning of everyday life. Wilder, though not a Christian, leads his characters to find significance in traditional values.

Fill in each of the blanks using items from the following word list:

novel	novelist	Yale
Our Town	playwright	reproduced
Princeton	reality	traditional
World War II	scenery	unconventional

3.16   Thornton Wilder was a successful _____ and _____, earning three Pulitzer Prizes.

3.17   Wilder earned his bachelor's degree from _____ and his master's degree from _____ .

3.18   He served as an officer in both World War I and _____ .

3.19   In 1928 Wilder earned his first Pulitzer Prize for his _____, *The Bridge at San Luis Rey.*

3.20   Wilder's play, _____ , earned him a second Pulitzer Prize.

3.21   No curtains and little _____ are used in Wilder's plays, making them _____ .

3.22   Wilder never wanted his audience to forget that the play they were watching was not _____ .

3.23   *Our Town* is one of Wilder's most _____ plays.

3.24   Wilder's characters often find significance in _____ values.

What to Look For:

Thornton Wilder's plays are unusual. They use little, if any, scenery. A character known as the Stage Manager interprets the play for the audience. As you read the following play, notice the role of the stage manager. How does the role of the Stage Manager shape the play?

*Please read *Our Town* by Thornton Wilder, available through Alpha Omega Publications or your local library.

Answer *true* or *false* for each of the following statements.

3.25   _____   The stage directions of Wilder's plays call for an elaborate curtain.

3.26   _____   Rebecca introduces the play to the audience.

3.27   _____   The Stage Manager tells the audience that in the future Joe Crowell Jr. dies in France during the war.

3.28   _____   Mrs. Gibbs complains to her husband that George isn't chopping wood for her.

3.29   _____   Professor Willard answers questions about the population from the audience.

3.30 _____ Mr. Webb describes Grover's Corners as a very ordinary town.

3.31 _____ Mr. Webb tells the "Lady in a Box" that there is a lot of culture in Grover's Corners.

3.32 _____ Emily asks her mother if she is smart enough to get people interested.

3.33 _____ Emily's mother tells her that she is "pretty enough for all normal purposes."

3.34 _____ The Stage Manager wants to get a copy of the play placed in the cornerstone of the new bank so that people a thousand years from now will know a few simple facts about Grover's Corners.

3.35 _____ George wants to become a doctor like his father.

3.36 _____ After choir practice, the women stay late to gossip about Simon Stimson's drinking problem.

3.37 _____ Dr. Gibbs concludes that Simon Stimson drinks because he is not made for big-city life.

3.38 _____ Rebecca tells her brother about the unusual address on an envelope.

3.39 _____ George announces the end of the first act.

RELIGIOUS WORKS

J. Gresham Machen (1881–1937). When J. Gresham Machen died in 1937, much of evangelical Protestantism in America sensed a great loss. As a defender of the faith and an advocate of the inerrancy of Scripture, he was fundamentalism's "most prominent champion" in the 1930s. His crusade of letters against the onslaught of liberal Protestantism helped to establish denominations and organizations committed to the orthodox Christian faith.

John Gresham Machen was born in Baltimore, Maryland. In 1901 he graduated from John Hopkins University. Unsure of his calling, Machen continued his studies at Princeton Theological Seminary. He took several academic trips to Europe and studied at Marburg University in Germany. In 1906 he returned to Princeton to teach New Testament theology. He remained at Princeton until 1929.

Machen began his career as a writer with the publication of his message "Christianity and Culture" in 1912. His defense of Christianity against the modernists (liberal Protestants) made him popular among conservative Christians. He was a hero of fundamentalists because he insisted upon the historical truthfulness of the Bible and was unwilling to compromise on the question of supernatural events (i.e., miracles). He said that the Bible is "a plain book addressed to plain men, and it means exactly what it says." As a respected scholar, his arguments gave much credence to the conservative stance upon the harmony of Christianity and science. Those who believed that the theory of evolution denied the truthfulness of Scripture were comforted by his fitly spoken words. He stood directly opposed to those within Protestantism that sought to do away with the idea of sin and the individual's need of a Savior.

His most well-known book, *Christianity and Liberalism,* published in 1923, argued that modernists were not preaching the gospel but had created a new religion. His thorough yet plain examination of the differences between modernism and Christianity won him the respect of secular intellectuals but failed to return wayward denominations to the fundamentals of the faith. Machen's application of truth is as beneficial today as it was in the 1920s and 1930s.

3.40   As an advocate of the (inaccuracy, inerrancy, myth) of Scripture, J. Gresham Machen was (liberalism's, fundamentalism's, modernism's) "most prominent champion" in the 1930s.

3.41   Machen taught New Testament theology at (Harvard, John Hopkins, Princeton) Theological Seminary.

3.42   Machen defended orthodox (Islam, Christianity, Judaism) against the onslaught of (conservative, liberal) Protestantism.

3.43   *Christianity and Liberalism,* Machen's most well-known book, argued that (fundamentalists, modernists) were not preaching the gospel but had created a new religion.

3.44   Machen's writing won the respect of (German theologians, secular intellectuals, liberal Protestants).

What to Look For:

J. Gresham Machen argued that liberal Protestants or modernists were preaching another gospel. In an attempt to be like the modern age, they had created another religion. As you read the following selection, examine carefully the differences between the Christian gospel and the message of liberal Protestantism. What are the significant differences? How important is history to the gospel? What do modernists believe is the way to heaven? Is liberal Protestantism really a new religion?

The following sections are excerpts from the book.

From: Christianity & Liberalism by J. Gresham Machen (1923)

Introduction:

The great redemptive religion which has always been known as Christianity is battling against a totally diverse type of religious belief, which is only the more destructive of the Christian faith because it makes use of traditional Christian terminology. This modern non-redemptive religion is called "modernism" or "liberalism."

The liberal attempt at reconciling Christianity with modern science has really relinquished everything distinctive of Christianity, so that what remains is in essentials only that same indefinite type of religious aspiration which was in the world before Christianity came upon the scene. In trying to remove from Christianity everything that could possibly be objected to in the name of science, in trying to bribe off the enemy by those concessions which the enemy most desires, the apologist has really abandoned what he started out to defend.

In view of the lamentable defects of modern life, a type of religion certainly should not be commended simply because it is modern or condemned simply because it is old. In the midst of all the material achievements of modern life, one may well ask the question whether in gaining the whole world we have not lost our own soul. Are we forever condemned to live the sordid life of utilitarianism? Or is there some lost secret which if rediscovered will restore to mankind something of the glories of the past?

Such a secret the writer of this little book would discover in the Christian religion. But the Christian religion which is meant is certainly not the religion of the modern liberal church, but a message of divine grace.

From: Chapter 3, God & Man

The Christian gospel consists in an account of how God saved man, and before that gospel can be understood something must be known (1) about God and (2) about man. The doctrine of God and the doctrine of man are the two great presuppositions of the gospel. With regard to these presuppositions, as with regard to the gospel itself, modern liberalism is diametrically opposed to Christianity.

It is opposed to Christianity, in the first place, in its conception of God. But at this point we are met with a particularly insistent form of that objection to doctrinal matters which has already been considered. It is unnecessary, we are told, to have a "conception" of God; theology, or the knowledge of God, it is said, is the death of religion; we should not seek to know God, but should merely feel His presence.

With regard to this objection, it ought to be observed that if religion consists merely in feeling the presence of God, it is devoid of any moral quality whatever. Pure feeling, if there be such a thing, is non-moral. What makes affection for a human friend, for example, such an ennobling thing is the knowledge which we possess of the character of our friend. Human affection, apparently so simple, is really just bristling with dogma. It depends upon a host of observations treasured up in the mind with regard to the character of our friends. But if human affection is thus really dependent upon knowledge, why should it be otherwise with that supreme personal relationship which is at the basis of religion? Why should we be indignant about slanders directed against a human friend, while at the same time we are patient about the basest slanders directed against our God? Certainly it does make the greatest possible difference what we think about God; the knowledge of God is the very basis of religion.

Christianity differs from liberalism, then, in the first place, in its conception of God. But it also differs in its conception of man. Modern liberalism has lost all sense of the gulf that separates the creature from the Creator; its doctrine of man

follows naturally from its doctrine of God. But it is not only the creature limitations of mankind which are denied. Even more important is another difference. According to the Bible, man is a sinner under the just condemnation of God; according to modern liberalism, there is really no such thing as sin. At the very root of the modern liberal movement is the loss of the consciousness of sin.

The consciousness of sin was formerly the starting-point of all preaching; but today it is gone. Characteristic of the modern age, above all else, is a supreme confidence in human goodness; the religious literature of the day is redolent of that confidence. Get beneath the rough exterior of men, we are told, and we shall discover enough self-sacrifice to found upon it the hope of society; the world's evil, it is said, can be overcome with the world's good; no help is needed from outside the world.

What has produced this satisfaction with human goodness? What has become of the consciousness of sin? The consciousness of sin has certainly been lost. But what has removed it from the hearts of men?

In the first place, the war has perhaps had something to do with the change. In time of war, our attention is called so exclusively to the sins of other people that we are sometimes inclined to forget our own sins. Attention to the sins of other people is, indeed, sometimes necessary. It is quite right to be indignant against any oppression of the weak which is being carried on by the strong. But such a habit of mind, if made permanent, if carried over into the days of peace, has its dangers. It joins forces with the collectivism of the modern state to obscure the individual, personal character of guilt. If John Smith beats his wife nowadays, no one is so old-fashioned as to blame John Smith for it. On the contrary, it is said, John Smith is evidently the victim of some more of that Bolshevistic propaganda; Congress ought to be called in extra session in order to take up the case of John Smith in an alien and sedition law.

But the loss of the consciousness of sin is far deeper than the war; it has its roots in a mighty spiritual process which has been active during the past seventy-five years. Like other great movements, that process has come silently—so silently that its results have been achieved before the plain man was even aware of what was taking place. Nevertheless, despite all superficial continuity, a remarkable change has come about within the last seventy-five years. The change is nothing less than the substitution of paganism for Christianity as the dominant view of life. Seventy-five years ago, Western civilization, despite inconsistencies, was still predominantly Christian; today it is predominantly pagan.

What, then, is paganism? The answer is not really difficult. Paganism is that view of life which finds the highest goal of human existence in the healthy and harmonious and joyous development of existing human faculties. Very different is the Christian ideal. Paganism is optimistic with regard to unaided human nature, whereas Christianity is the religion of the broken heart.

In saying that Christianity is the religion of the broken heart, we do not mean that Christianity ends with the broken heart; we do not mean that the characteristic Christian attitude is a continual beating on the breast or a continual crying of "Woe is me." Nothing could be further from the fact. On the contrary, Christianity means that sin is faced once for all, and then is cast, by the grace of God, forever into the depths of the sea—In Christianity, on the other hand, nothing needs to be covered up. The fact of sin is faced squarely once for all, and is dealt with by the grace of God. But then, after sin has been removed by the grace of God, the Christian can proceed to develop joyously every faculty that God has given him. Such is the higher Christian humanism—a humanism founded not upon human pride but upon divine grace.

But although Christianity does not end with the broken heart, it does begin with the broken heart; it begins with the consciousness of sin. Without the consciousness of sin, the whole of the gospel will seem to be an idle tale. But how can the consciousness of sin be revived? Something no doubt can be accomplished by the proclamation of the law of God, for the law reveals transgressions. The whole of the law, moreover, should be proclaimed.

The fundamental fault of the modern Church is that she is busily engaged in an absolutely impossible task—she is busily engaged in calling the righteous to repentance. Modern preachers are trying to bring men into the Church without requiring them to relinquish their pride; they are trying to help men avoid the conviction of sin. The preacher gets up into the pulpit, opens the Bible, and addresses the congregation somewhat as follows: "You people are very good," he says; "you respond to every appeal that looks toward the welfare of the community. Now we have in the Bible—especially in the life of Jesus—something so good that we believe it is good enough even for you good people." Such is modern preaching. It is heard every Sunday in thousands of pulpits. But it is entirely futile. Even our Lord did not call the righteous to repentance, and probably we shall be no more successful than He.

From: Chapter 4, "The Bible"

According to the Christian view, the Bible contains an account of a revelation from God to man, which is found nowhere else. It is true, the Bible also contains a confirmation and a wonderful enrichment of the revelations which are given also by the things that God has made and by the conscience of man. "The heavens declare the glory of God; and the firmament showeth his handywork"—these words are a confirmation of the revelation of God in nature; "all have sinned and fall short of the glory of God"—these words are a confirmation of what is attested by the conscience. But in addition to such reaffirmations of what might conceivably be learned elsewhere—as a matter of fact, because of men's blindness, even so much is learned elsewhere only in comparatively obscure fashion—the Bible also contains an account of a revelation which is absolutely new. That new revelation concerns the way by which sinful man can come into communion with the living God.

The way was opened, according to the Bible, by an act of God, when, almost nineteen hundred years ago, outside the walls of Jerusalem, the eternal Son was offered as a sacrifice for the sins of men. To that one great event the whole Old Testament looks forward, and in that one event the whole of the New Testament finds its center and core. Salvation then, according to the Bible, is not something that was discovered, but something that happened. Hence appears the uniqueness of the Bible. All the ideas of Christianity might be discovered in some other religion, yet there would be in that other religion no Christianity. For Christianity depends, not upon a complex of ideas, but upon the narration of an event. Without that event, the world, in the Christian view, is altogether dark, and humanity is lost under the guilt of sin. There can be no salvation by the discovery of eternal truth, for eternal truth brings naught but despair, because of sin. But a new face has been put upon life by the blessed thing that God did when He offered up His only begotten Son.

An objection is sometimes offered against this view of the contents of the Bible. Must we, it is said, depend upon what happened so long ago? Does salvation wait upon the examination of musty records? Is the trained student of Palestinian history the modern priest without whose gracious intervention no one can see God? Can we not find, instead, a salvation that is independent of history, a salvation that depends only on what is with us here and now?

The objection is not devoid of weight. But it ignores one of the primary evidences for the truth of the gospel record. That evidence is found in Christian experience.

Salvation does depend upon what happened long ago, but the event of long ago has effects that continue until today. We are told in the New Testament that Jesus offered Himself as a sacrifice for the sins of those who should believe on Him. That is a record of a past event. But we can make trial of it today, and making trial of it we find it to be true. We are told in the New Testament that on a certain morning long ago Jesus rose from the dead. That again is a record of a past event. But again we can make trial of it, and making trial of it we discover that Jesus is truly a living Savior today.

But at this point a fatal error lies in wait. It is one of the root errors of modern liberalism. Christian experience, we have just said, is useful as confirming the gospel message. But because it is necessary, many men have jumped to the conclusion that it is all that is necessary. Having a present experience of Christ in the heart, may we not, it is said, hold that experience no matter what history may tell us as to the events of the first Easter morning? May we not make ourselves altogether independent of the results of Biblical criticism? No matter what sort of man history may tell us Jesus of Nazareth actually was, no matter what history may say about the real meaning of His death or about the story of His alleged resurrection, may we not continue to experience the presence of Christ in our souls?

The trouble is that the experience thus maintained is not Christian experience. Religious experience it may be, but Christian experience it certainly is not. For Christian experience depends absolutely upon an event. The Christian says to himself: "I have meditated upon the problem of becoming right with God, I have tried to produce a righteousness that will stand in His sight; but when I heard the gospel message I learned that what I had weakly striven to accomplish had been accomplished by the Lord Jesus Christ when He died for me on the Cross and completed His redeeming work by the glorious resurrection. If the thing has not yet been done, if I merely have an idea of its accomplishment, then I am of all men most miserable, for I am still in my sins. My Christian life, then, depends altogether upon the truth of the New Testament record."

Christian experience is rightly used when it confirms the documentary evidence. But it can never possibly provide a substitute for the documentary evidence. We know that the gospel story is true partly because of the early date of the documents in which it appears, the evidence as to their authorship, the internal evidence of their truth, the impossibility of explaining them as being based upon deception or upon myth. This evidence is gloriously confirmed by present experience, which adds to the documentary evidence that wonderful directness and immediacy of conviction which delivers us from fear. Christian experience is rightly used when it helps to convince us that the events narrated in the New Testament actually did occur; but it can never enable us to be Christians whether the events occurred or not. It is a fair flower, and should be prized as a gift of God. But cut it from its root in the blessed Book, and it soon withers away and dies....

What is the liberal view as to the seat of authority in religion?

The impression is sometimes produced that the modern liberal substitutes for the authority of the Bible the authority of Christ. He cannot accept, he says, what he regards as the perverse moral teaching of the Old Testament or the sophistical arguments of Paul. But he regards himself as being the true Christian because, rejecting the rest of the Bible, he depends upon Jesus alone.

This impression, however, is utterly false. The modern liberal does not really hold to the authority of Jesus. Even if he did so, indeed, he would still be impoverishing greatly his knowledge of God and of the way of salvation....

The real authority, for liberalism, can only be "the Christian consciousness" or "Christian experience." But how shall the findings of the Christian consciousness be established? Surely not by a majority vote of the organized Church. Such a method would obviously do away with all liberty of conscience. The only authority, then, can be individual experience; truth can only be that which "helps" the individual man. Such an authority is obviously no authority at all; for individual experience is endlessly diverse, and when once truth is regarded only as that which works at any particular time, it ceases to be truth. The result is an abysmal skepticism.

The Christian man, on the other hand, finds in the Bible the very Word of God. Let it not be said that dependence upon a book is a dead or an artificial thing. The Reformation of the sixteenth century was founded upon the authority of the Bible, yet it set the world aflame. Dependence upon a word of man would be slavish, but dependence upon God's word is life. Dark and gloomy would be the world, if we were left to our own devices and had no blessed Word of God. The Bible, to the Christian is not a burdensome law, but the very Magna Charta of Christian liberty.

It is no wonder, then, that liberalism is totally different from Christianity, for the foundation is different. Christianity is founded upon the Bible. It bases upon the Bible both its thinking and its life. Liberalism, on the other hand, is founded upon the shifting emotions of sinful men.

It has been observed thus far that liberalism differs from Christianity with regard to the presuppositions of the gospel (the view of God and the view of man), with regard to the Book in which the gospel is contained, and with regard to the Person whose work the gospel sets forth. It is not surprising then that it differs from Christianity in its account of the gospel itself; it is not surprising that it presents an entirely different account of the way of salvation. Liberalism finds salvation (so far as it is willing to speak at all of "salvation") in man; Christianity finds it in an act of God.

The difference with regard to the way of salvation concerns, in the first place, the basis of salvation in the redeeming work of Christ. According to Christian belief, Jesus is our Savior, not by virtue of what He said, not even by virtue of what He was, but by what He did. He is our Savior, not because He has inspired us to live the same kind of life that He lived, but because He took upon Himself the dreadful guilt of our sins and bore it instead of us on the cross. Such is the Christian conception of the Cross of Christ. It is ridiculed as being a "subtle theory of the atonement." In reality, it is the plain teaching of the word of God; we know absolutely nothing about an atonement that is not a vicarious atonement, for that is the only atonement of which the New Testament speaks. And this Bible doctrine is not intricate or subtle. On the contrary, though it involves mysteries, it is itself so simple that a child can understand it. "We deserved eternal death, but the Lord Jesus, because He loved us, died instead of us on the cross"—surely there is nothing so very intricate about that. It is not the Bible doctrine of the atonement which is difficult to understand—what are really incomprehensible are the elaborate modern efforts to get rid of the Bible doctrine in the interests of human pride.

It is true that the Christian gospel is an account, not of something that happened yesterday, but of something that happened long ago; but the important thing is that it really happened. If it really happened, then it makes little difference when it happened. No matter when it happened, whether yesterday or in the first century, it remains a real gospel, a real piece of news.

But as a matter of fact the modern objection to the doctrine of the atonement on the ground that doctrine is contrary to the love of God, is based upon the most abysmal misunderstanding of the doctrine itself. The modern liberal teachers persist in speaking of the sacrifice of Christ as though it were a sacrifice made by some one other than God. They speak of it as though it meant that God waits coldly until a price is paid to Him before He forgives sin. As a matter of fact, it means nothing of the kind; the objection ignores that which is absolutely fundamental in the Christian doctrine of the Cross. The fundamental thing is that God Himself, and not another, makes the sacrifice for sin—God Himself in the person of the Son who assumed our nature and died for us, God Himself in the Person of the Father who spared not His own Son but offered Him up for us all. Salvation is as free for us as the air we breathe; God's the dreadful cost, ours the gain. "God so loved the world that He gave His only begotten Son." Such love is very different from the complacency found in the God of modern preaching; this love is love that did not count the cost; it is love that is love indeed.

At the center of Christianity is the doctrine of "justification by faith." In exalting faith, we are not immediately putting ourselves in contradiction to modern thought. Indeed faith is being exalted very high by men of the most modern type. But what kind of faith? There emerges the difference of opinion.

Faith is being exalted so high today that men are being satisfied with any kind of faith, just so it is faith. It makes no difference what is believed, we are told, just so the blessed attitude of faith is there. The undogmatic faith, it is said, is better than the dogmatic, because it is purer faith—faith less weakened by the alloy of knowledge.

Faith is so very useful, they tell us, that we must not scrutinize its basis in truth. But, the great trouble is, such an avoidance of scrutiny itself involves the destruction of faith. For faith is essentially dogmatic. Despite all you can do, you cannot remove the element of intellectual assent from it. Faith is the opinion that some person will do something for you. If that person really will do that thing for you, then the faith is true. If he will not do it, then the faith is false. In the latter case, not all the benefits in the world will make the faith true. Though it has transformed the world from darkness to light, though it has produced thousands of glorious healthy lives, it remains a pathological phenomenon. It is false, and sooner or later it is sure to be found out.

Such counterfeits should be removed, not out of a love of destruction, but in order to leave room for the pure gold, the existence of which is implied in the presence of the counterfeits. Faith is often based upon error, but there would be no faith at all unless it were sometimes based upon truth. But if Christian faith is based upon truth, then it is not the faith which saves the Christian but the object of the faith. And the object of the faith is Christ. Faith, then, according to the Christian view means simply receiving a gift. To have faith in Christ means to cease trying to win God's favor by one's own character; the man who believes in Christ simply accepts the sacrifice which Christ offered on Calvary. The result of such faith is a new life and all good works; but the salvation itself is an absolutely free gift of God.

Very different is the conception of faith which prevails in the liberal Church. According to modern liberalism, faith is essentially the same as "making Christ Master" in one's life; at least it is by making Christ Master in the life that the welfare of men is sought. But that simply means that salvation is thought to be obtained by our own obedience to the commands of Christ. Such teaching is just a sublimated form of legalism. Not the sacrifice of Christ, on this view, but our own obedience to God's law, is the ground of hope.

In this way the whole achievement of the Reformation has been given up, and there has been a return to the religion of the Middle Ages. At the beginning of the sixteenth century, God raised up a man who began to read the Epistle to the Galatians with his own eyes. The result was the rediscovery of the doctrine of justification by faith. Upon that rediscovery has been based the whole of our evangelical freedom. As expounded by Luther and Calvin the Epistle to the Galatians became the "Magna Charta of Christian liberty." But modern liberalism has returned to the old interpretation of Galatians which was urged against the Reformers.

The grace of God is rejected by modern liberalism. And the result is slavery—the slavery of the law, the wretched bondage by which man undertakes the impossible task of establishing his own righteousness as a ground of acceptance with God. It may seem strange at first sight that "liberalism," of which the very name means freedom, should in reality be wretched slavery. But the phenomenon is not really so strange. Emancipation from the blessed will of God always involves bondage to some worse taskmaster.

Answer *true* or *false* for each of the following statements.

3.45 _____ Christianity is the "great redemptive religion."

3.46 _____ The Christian gospel is an account of how man saves himself.

3.47 _____ Pure feeling is nonmoral.

3.48 _____ The knowledge of God is the very basis of religion.

3.49 _____ Liberalism and Christianity have identical concepts of God and man.

3.50 _____ Liberalism does not have a concept of sin.

3.51 _____ Christianity is similar to paganism in its optimistic view of man.

3.52 _____ Liberalism faces sin squarely and deals with it by the grace of God.

3.53 _____ Christianity begins with the consciousness of sin.

3.54 _____ Salvation, according to the Bible, depends upon an event that happened long ago.

3.55 _____ According to liberalism, the Christian life depends altogether upon the truth of the New Testament record.

3.56 _____ Liberalism is founded upon the shifting emotions of sinful men, otherwise known as "experience."

3.57 _____ Christianity finds salvation in man.

3.58 _____ According to Christianity, Jesus is our Savior by virtue of what He did.

3.59 _____ At the center of liberalism is the doctrine of "justification by faith."

3.60 _____ According to Christianity, faith is essentially the same as "making Christ Master" in one's life.

3.61 _____ Liberalism says that our obedience to God's law is the ground of hope.

3.62 _____ Modern liberalism rejects the grace of God

3.63 _____ "Liberalism," because it requires that men establish their own righteousness as grounds for acceptance with God, is in reality a wretched slavery.

Before you take this last Self-Test, you might want to do one or more of the following self-checks.

1. _____ Read the objectives. Determine if you can do them.

2. _____ Restudy the material related to any objectives that you cannot do.

3. _____ Use the **SQ3R** study procedure to review the material:

    a. **S**can the sections.
    b. **Q**uestion yourself again (review the questions you wrote initially).
    c. **R**ead to answer your questions.
    d. **R**ecite the answers to yourself.
    e. **R**eview areas that you didn't understand.

4. _____ Review all vocabulary, activities, and Self-Tests, writing a correct answer for each answer you got wrong.

SELF-TEST 3

Fill in each of the blanks using items from the following word list (each answer, 3 points).

unconventional	hero	scenery
cultural	reality	clear
novelist	American	religion
playwright	emptiness	rhythm
satire		

3.01   Ernest Hemingway's writing style is _____ and precise.

3.02   F. Scott Fitzgerald's characters are troubled by an _____ they cannot fill.

3.03   Unable to find an answer to the world's problems in politics, W.H. Auden turned to _____ .

3.04   "The Unknown Citizen" is a _____ of modern problems.

3.05   The poetry of Langston Hughes captures the _____ of jazz and blues.

3.06   Jesse B. Semple became a black folk _____ .

3.07   Hughes inspired other black writers to take pride in their _____ roots.

3.08   Hughes's work helped to provide a lasting place for black writers in _____ literature.

3.09   Thornton Wilder was a successful _____ and _____ , earning three Pulitzer Prizes.

3.010   Curtains and _____ are not used in Wilder's plays, making them _____ .

3.011   Wilder never wanted his audience to forget that the play they were watching was not _____ .

Answer *true* or *false* for each of the following statements (each answer, 1 point).

3.012   _____   World War I proved that society and its traditional beliefs and manners had failed.

3.013   _____   After World War I, art began to reflect the pessimism and discontinuity of the modern age.

3.014   _____   Modernism assumed that the world had moved into a post-Christian era.

3.015   _____   Faces are compared to petals on a tree branch in the poem "In a Station of the Metro."

3.016   _____   In his poem "Chicago," Carl Sandburg uses long lines of free verse.

3.017   _____   In *"r-p-o-p-h-e-s-s-a-g-r"* the word *bug* is scrambled three times.

3.018   _____   In the poem, "Anecdote of the Jar," the jar shapes reality.

3.019   _____   In Frost's poem, "Mending Wall," the neighbor's only response to the speaker is, "Good fences make good neighbors."

3.020   _____   In "The Unknown Citizen," W.H. Auden is criticizing modern society because it is too personal.

3.021   _____   In "The Trumpet Player," the phrase "The Negro/ with the trumpet at his lips" is repeated in stanzas 1, 2, and 5.

3.022 _____ The music is described as "honey/ Mixed with liquid fire."

3.023 _____ The rhythm is described as "agony/ Distilled from new desire."

3.024 _____ In the play *"Our Town,"* the stage directions call for an elaborate curtain.

3.025 _____ The Stage Manager tells the audience that in the future Joe Crowell, Jr. dies in France during the war.

3.026 _____ Mr. Webb describes Grover's Corners as a very ordinary town.

3.027 _____ Emily's mother tells her that she is "pretty enough for all normal purposes."

3.028 _____ The Stage Manager wants to get a copy of the play placed in the cornerstone of the new bank so that people a thousand years from now will know a few simple facts about Grover's Corners.

3.029 _____ George announces the end of the first act in *"Our Town."*

3.030 _____ The Christian gospel is an account of how man saves himself.

3.031 _____ The knowledge of God is the very basis of religion.

3.032 _____ Liberalism and Christianity have identical concepts of God and man.

3.033 _____ Christianity is similar to paganism in its optimistic view of man.

3.034 _____ Liberalism faces sin squarely and deals with it by the grace of God.

3.035 _____ Christianity begins with the consciousness of sin.

3.036 _____ Salvation, according to the Bible, depends upon an event that happened long ago.

3.037 _____ Liberalism is founded upon the shifting emotions of sinful men, otherwise known as "experience."

3.038 _____ At the center of liberalism is the doctrine of "justification by faith."

3.039 _____ Liberalism says that our obedience to God's law is the ground of hope.

3.040 _____ Modern liberalism rejects the grace of God.

Underline the correct answer in each of the following statements (each answer, 2 points).

3.041 The modernist style (expands, exaggerates, compresses) emotion and narration.

3.042 The modernist movement saw truth as a matter of (biblical standard, historical record, interpretation).

3.043 Black writers of the Harlem Renaissance carried the rhythms of (baroque, classical, jazz and blues) music over into various forms of literature.

3.044 Ezra Pound's experimental techniques and forms had no regard for (traditional, modern, progressive) ideas and approaches.

3.045 Pound's most influential form of poetry was called (traditionalism, imagism, communism).

3.046 Imagism focused on concrete (impressions, images, types) rather than abstractions.

3.047 Carl Sandburg wrote about the struggles and triumphs of the (middle, working, upper) class.

3.048 E.E. Cummings used (traditional, experimental, orthodox) forms to view the familiar in a new way.

3.049 Wallace Stevens believed that (worship, poetry, singing) was the highest human activity.

3.050 As a traditional poet, Frost believed that poetry should begin in (pain, agony, delight) and end with (wisdom, confusion, ignorance).

3.051 As an advocate of the (inaccuracy, inerrancy, myth) of Scripture, J. Gresham Machen was (liberalism's, fundamentalism's, modernism's) "most prominent champion" in the 1930s.

3.052 Machen defended orthodox (Islam, Christianity, Judaism) against the onslaught of (conservative, liberal) Protestantism.

3.053 *Christianity and Liberalism,* Machen's most well-known book, argued that (fundamentalists, modernists) were not preaching the gospel but had created a new religion.

For Thought and Discussion

Explain to a parent or teacher the controversy between the fundamentalists and the modernists (liberal Protestants). Be sure to give a brief summary of J. Gresham Machen's comparison of Christianity and liberalism. Your summary should include the different views of God, man, and the way of salvation. Discuss the importance of the Bible in determining both what the Christian faith is and what it is not.

Score _____

Teacher check _____

Initial   Date

 Before taking the LIFEPAC Test, you might want to do one or more of the following self-checks.

1. _____ Read the objectives. Check to see if you can do them.

2. _____ Restudy the material related to any objectives that you cannot do.

3. _____ Use the **SQ3R** study procedure to review the material.

4. _____ Review activities, Self-Tests, and LIFEPAC vocabulary words.

5. _____ Restudy areas of weakness indicated by the previous Self-Test.